AT ONE FOREVER

Mystical Adventures Into Oneness

Geneviève Lucette

Hapi Publications
© 2012 by Geneviève Lucette
www.atoneforever.com
Cover photograph of author by Bobby

Dedication

This book is dedicated to You, the seeker of Truth,
For the love in your heart is the light of this world.

*

My gratitude goes to Raymond Bernard and
Peter Dawkins for the work they accomplished
In serving the Greater Light.

*

I am grateful to my family and friends
For their love and support
That resulted in the gift of this book.

Contents

Introduction ... 6
Meaning of Words ... 8

Chapter 1

Rendez-Vous with Destiny ... 10

Chapter 2

Universal Life & Interplay ... 33
The Crowned Ibis ... 34
Creative Power ... 39
The Awakening Angel ... 42
Rainbow Around the Sun ... 44
The Mystical Leonardo da Vinci ... 49

Chapter 3

The Holographic Universe ... 58
Gateway & Gatekeeper ... 68
Master Souls ... 73
Star Light ... 75
2012 & Beyond ... 77
Freedom ... 82

Appendix 1 - The Wheel of Time & Space ... 86
Appendix 2 - The Emerald Tablet Exercise ... 91
Appendix 3 - The Baconian Keyboard ... 94

Photographs by Geneviève Lucette

Golden Dawn ... 14
At One Forever ... 17
Key of Life ... 22
Soul of Light ... 25
Light & Matter ... 29
Rose in Sands of Time ... 30
The Crowned Ibis ... 34
Birds Interplay ... 40
The Awakening Angel ... 43
Rainbow Around the Sun ... 45
Pyramid of Light ... 67
Face in the Cloud ... 75

Illustrations

Orion & Sirius ... 12
Orion & Sirius and the Pyramids ... 13
Circles within Circles ... 23
The Universal Man of Light ... 51
Star of David ... 53
The Flower of Life ... 53
The Golden Ratio ... 54
Fleur de Lys ... 55
The Gatekeeper ... 69
The Wheel of Time & Space ... 87
The Waves of Time ... 88
The Emerald Tablet Exercise ... 91
The Baconian Keyboard ... 95

*The most beautiful and most profound experience
Is the sensation of the mystical.*

It is the sower of all true science.

He to whom this emotion is a stranger,

Who can no longer wonder

And stand rap in awe, is as good as dead."

~Albert Einstein

Introduction

Youthful inspiration led me to a fascination about the mysteries of life and my own mystery. I wanted to know what love was and what life was all about. Then, unexpectedly, the opportunity to study the mysteries of life presented itself. I received the benefit of tutelage from Western Wisdom Traditions particularly from the Rosicrucians-Amorc and the Francis Bacon Research Trust. To my delight, their teachings covered the Ancient Egyptian and the Christian Mysteries in a philosophical and mystical way. Within this milieu, I had a series of mystical experiences and recognized my Divinity, the very core of what I truly am.

The ideal of a mystic is to develop a direct and intimate awareness of God within, in Nature, and the Universe. The beauty of Mysticism is in its universality. Mysticism is an art and a science of life. It is an art of living because it allows us to express our own Divinity. As a science, it teaches us about natural and spiritual laws of life. When we have an understanding of these laws, we can then apply them to promote health, happiness, prosperity, and peace in our lives and in the world.

The title of this book 'At One Forever' was inspired by the ancient Egyptian name of Aton. Thirty-three hundred years ago, Pharaoh Akhenaton revealed for the first time the name of the One God as Aton – the Absolute Being. Aton is the root of the English word atonement – at-one-ment or at-one-ness. In mystical practices, the term 'at-one' refers to the unification of Spirit, Soul, and Body.

Rather than approaching the mysteries of life and the realm of the Soul in an abstract way, I will be sharing with you a mystical way to participate in the mysteries of life. This practical approach stimulates a sacred dimension of life that is rewarding and freeing. The word 'mystery' refers to a play in which profound truths about ourselves and the Universe can be discovered. *"All the world's a stage, and all the men and women merely players."* Shakespeare.

Throughout the book, I will recount some of my mystical adventures. Twelve photographs are presented in the book which captured archetypal symbols and myths. Just before I began my first spiritual retreat in 1996, I translated the ancient Egyptian 'Emerald Tablet' knowing that it was an alchemical formula for regeneration. I converted it into an exercise, a series of gentle movements to establish balance and harmony within and reinforce my aura. To decode letters, numbers, and words I used the 'Baconian Keyboard' to receive confirmation, guidance and encouragement or even a signature. To research, decode, and follow the symbols and clues is to find oneself on an extraordinary treasure trail filled with excitements and delights. Knowing that my mystical experiences were synchronized with time, I followed diligently the Wheel of Time and Space. These three systems are introduced in the Appendixes 1, 2 and 3.

My most profound wish is that the book will assist and encourage you on your spiritual path. We are living in a momentous time in human history. As we approach, the famous and critical date of December 21, 2012 humanity's consciousness is being hasten into a higher level of consciousness and evolutionary state. As the world's transformation speeds up, we are experiencing a great cleansing and rebalancing on a personal, national, and global level. More than ever, it is important to keep our aura strong and remain centered in our own Soul.

Through this book, I am grateful for the opportunity to share with you a mystical way of experiencing life and the realm of the Soul. I now would like to invite you to join me on the journey into oneness.

* * *

Meaning of Words

Throughout the book, I use the words **Spirit, Soul, and Body** to refer to a different realm and mode of expression of Divinity. They are difficult words to use because they have many different and contradictory meanings for different people. For this reason, I would like to state clearly the meaning each one has for me.

Spirit is defined as the creative life force and life giving energy, the masculine aspect of Divinity. Spirit is known as the Christ, the Light of God that radiates forth from the divine Source. Spirit is Christ Consciousness known as the Word of God, Holy Breath, Holy Spirit, Wisdom, and Truth. The non-Christian mystics prefer the use of the term Cosmic Consciousness.

Soul is defined as the life form of Consciousness, the feminine aspect of Divinity. The Soul receives, manifests and makes visible the invisible Spirit. The Soul is the Holy Intelligence that gives form to the Spirit and manifests the Light so that the Spirit might be seen and known. Spirit dwells within the Soul. The two are inseparable soul mate complementing each other. They are One 'in love' for God is Love and the essence of oneness. The Soul is also known as the Universal

Mind, the Cosmos, Paradise, Beauty, or Bride. Sometimes the Soul is referred as the Kingdom. *"The kingdom of heaven is within."* The individual human Soul is an inseparable part of the Universal Soul of God.

The name **God** is used by the English translators of the Bible, which stands for various different names of the Absolute or Divine Being. The word 'God' is related to the word 'Good' and is a definition of the Absolute Being as the All-Goodness.

Body refers the material vehicle and the outermost mode of expression of Divinity. The term Spirit, Soul, and Body starts from the innermost mode of our Divinity. The mind, our intellect, is included in the term 'Body.' The human body with its cellular consciousness is a living form of intelligence. Our physical senses and objective consciousness create a sense of substantiality and reality. It is through the body and mind that the Soul manifests in the outer world.

Everything is energy. Every form of life is essentially an archetype or pattern of energy. The different aspects of a human being, Spirit, Soul and Body are made of vibratory energy. The frequency is what differentiates one manifestation from another. The physical body is simply a crystallized, dense and slowed down energy.

Chapter 1

Rendez-Vous with Destiny

My life changed completely in 1996. One morning as I was studying the nature of reality, an illustration of an ancient Egyptian mystic caught my attention. The mystic was a graceful lady dressed in a long white dress. She stood in front of the rising Sun with her arms outstretched, behind her on the ground lay the shadow of her body in the form of a cross. I wondered how she felt and what she saw thousands of years ago. What was she trying to tell me? As I pondered upon this multidimensional image, I recognized the three dimensions of the world and the fourth dimension of Time marked by the Sun. I was fascinated. I decided to follow her footsteps and stand up for myself in front of the rising Sun; little did I know that I had set myself on the incredible adventure of my life.

During the past decade, I had been immersed in my studies in Ancient Wisdom and now I was about to live an ancient mystery. I began to consider a place that would provide a peaceful atmosphere for a spiritual retreat. I chose a familiar place in Palm Beach, a small town on the eastern coast of Florida; I had no doubt that the timing had to coincide with the Egyptian New Year.

The ancient Egyptians were excellent astronomers; they recorded the solar cycle, lunar cycle and the Sothic cycle. The latter is based on the star Sirius when once a year at dawn it rises on the eastern horizon just before the Sun. The Egyptians used this conjunction to calculate the 365.25 days of the year and to mark the beginning of their New Year. Nowadays, we know Sirius as the Dog Star, the brightest star in the constellation of Canis Major. Using an astronomical software program, I found that according to today's calendar the heliacal rising of Sirius in Palm Beach would be on August $2^{nd.}$ I now had the place and the date for my first spiritual retreat.

With excitement, I reserved my seat on an airline and a room at the Heart of Palm Beach Hotel. For this special occasion, I bought a blue jean dress with a big eagle embroidered on its back. For me, an eagle in flight represents a new dimension of freedom. Symbolic images are relative and metaphoric. They represent a reality that relates to our psychological and spiritual worlds.

Upon arriving at the hotel, I settled in room number 110. Years later, I would discover the significance of this number in relation to my spiritual awakening. After unpacking, I went right away to the beach to find the perfect place for my alignment with the rising Sun. A flagpole caught my attention. It seemed to mark the perfect spot. "So be it!" I exclaimed. On my way back to the hotel, I bought a bouquet of twelve red roses to celebrate my first retreat and to put more beauty around me. I was aware that the red rose was not only the emblem of love but also of the Soul. That night, I went to bed early. I prayed for protection and asked God to keep my life as exciting as it was at that moment. I ended my prayer with gratitude for all that I had already received and would receive in the future. I fell asleep with a warm feeling of love in my heart.

During the night, I was awakened by a soft angelic voice calling my name. I did not question it. My mind stayed still in silence absorbing the subtle vibrations. I looked at the clock it was 3:30 in the morning. I knew that later on, I would decode this number to discover clues and find out who had called me and why. I was amazed but too sleepy to be excited. I awoke again at 6 o'clock and felt a strong urge to go to the beach before sunrise. It was still dark outside. The town was asleep with the exception of a few passing cars. I walked toward the flagpole and sat on a bench facing the eastern horizon. It felt strange to be at the beach at such an early hour, but I knew that I was following my intuition. I listened to the sounds of the breaking waves to keep my mind in the present moment. In the clear night sky, I gazed at the immensity of space and the magnificent display of stars. Each one shone forth in their stillness and glory, innumerable suns in profusion. In waiting for the sunrise, I had a prelude of the majesty of the Universe that gave me a sense of freedom and immortality. Wherever I gazed there was wonder. I was imbued with the beauty of the Universe. I recognized the constellations of Orion and Sirius that were so important to the ancient Egyptians. Orion was higher in the sky and seemed to be pointing to the rising of Sirius on the eastern horizon.

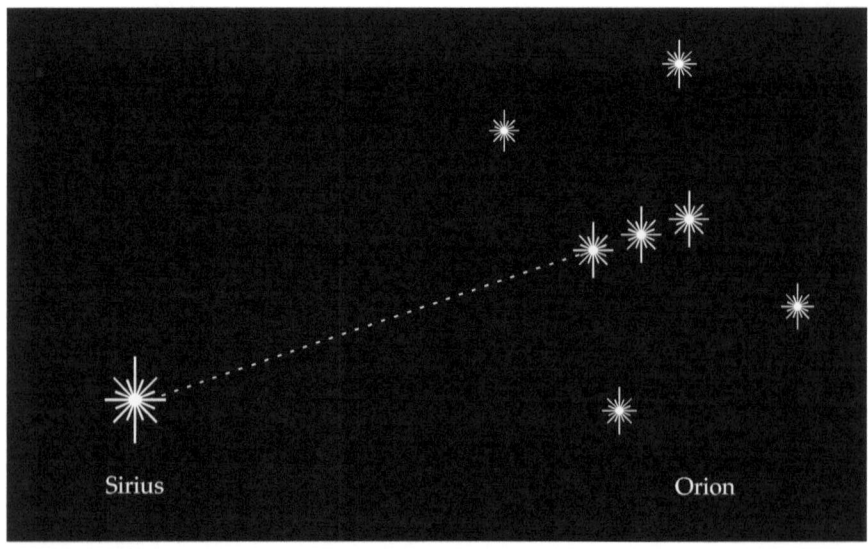

I remembered a fascinating book I read long ago called, 'The Message of the Sphinx,' by Graham Hancock and Robert Bauval in which they mentioned a connection between Orion and the pyramids at Giza. They stated that the three stars of Orion's belt matched perfectly the pattern of the three great pyramids on the ground.

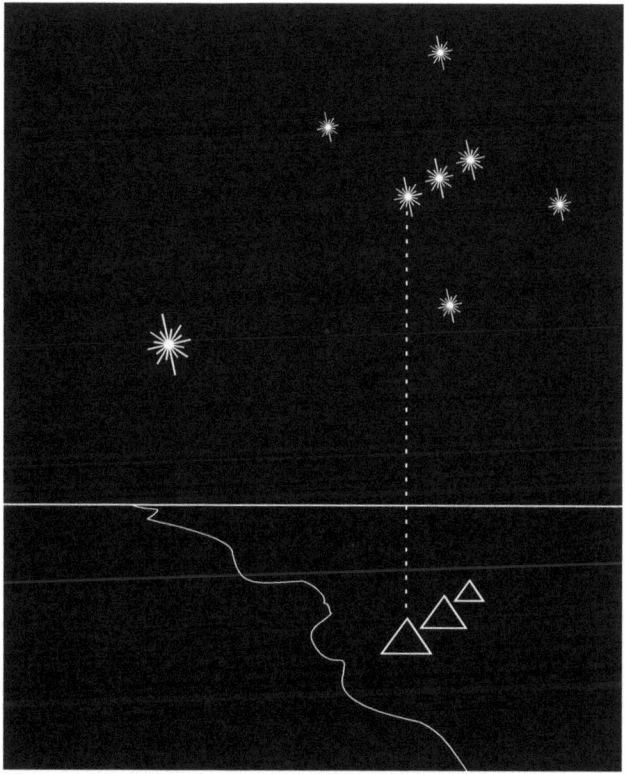

Years later, Robert Bauval wrote a new book called, 'The Egypt Code,' wherein he questioned the purpose of the pyramids at Giza, *"Why had the Egyptians sought to bring down to earth an image of the heavens?"* He went on to say that this special celestial alignment might have something to do with a universal time clock. The words: 'image', 'alignment' and 'universal time clock' resonated in my head. Indeed, the ancient Egyptian mystics were on their quest for Eternity. Did they find a way to connect with it, and if so how?

Slowly darkness dissipated and the stars faded away with the coming of the Sun. I strolled along the beach, the ocean was calm, the sky became reddish and golden. The morning silence filled the air with mystery.

Golden Dawn

I paused for a moment to reflect upon the symbolic image of the golden dawn. The law of Polarity between light and darkness was obvious. I recalled the words of Jesus when He said, *"I am the light of the world; he who follows me will not walk in darkness, but shall have the light of life."* Often Jesus used natural symbols to evoke abstract ideas and to teach universal laws and principles. Nature is God's Work that reveals divine qualities. Natural symbols are alive; they are never deceptive since they are living symbols of truth pointing the way toward enlightenment. To find the 'Way' of Jesus, we need to approach it with love and humility. The story of Jesus' life can be interpreted from different points of view, but the Light of Truth stands in freedom and transcends any human dogma, limited understanding, and spiritual vanity.

I continued contemplating the dawn light, when suddenly I realized that I was witnessing not only a new day, but also a re-enactment of the first day of Creation when God said, *"Let there be light."* I realized that the concept of the 7 days of Creation was linked to different systems: the spectrum of the 7 colors of the white light, the 7 notes of an octave of sound, the 7 chakras, the 7 planets and the 7 steps of initiation among others. My mind was like a scanner searching for the correspondences between these different systems.

I stopped thinking and paused for a moment. I simply looked at what was in front of me. I realized that I was seeing a symbolic language and a revelation. The Sun with its dawn light on the ocean gave allusion to a lighted candle and to the letter 'i.' In the Ancient Mystery Schools, the Masters often used the lighted candle to symbolize the three realms of Body, Soul and Spirit. The wax represented the Body, the flame revealed the Soul, the radiance and the warmth of the candle revealed the Spirit. The letter 'i' became an identification of a Presence for me. Within its geometric form number 1 became obvious. Together they gave me, 'I one' which could be read as, 'I am One' or 'I the One.' It was awe-inspiring to discover God's signature imprinted in the natural world and to enter a mystery. There is always a truth hidden under the under the illusion of appearances. This was my introduction to a new symbolic way of thinking that opened a channel of communication with my own Soul and the Soul of the Universe.

I recalled a quote from the Gospel of Philip, an early Christian text discovered at Nag in Egypt in which Jesus said:

"Truth did not come into the world naked,
But it came in types and images.
One will not receive truth in any other way
The bridegroom must enter through the image into the truth."

As I continued strolling along the beach toward the flagpole, my place of alignment, my focus was on the Sun sitting on the line of the horizon. It seemed to mark a conjunction point between Heaven and Earth. I was aware that I was journeying into the midst of a mystical realm that transcended time and space. Upon arriving, I prepared myself with prayers. I was now ready to let go of my reality and enter into the unknown. I stood up in front of the rising Sun with my arms outstretched and with the utmost reverence, I said aloud, *"Here I am. Let there be light."* Instantly in my heart I felt the gentle flutters of my Soul, an incredible excitement that gave me a deep appreciation of the sacred nature of life within me, within Nature and the Universe.

At One Forever

There in front of me was a narrow path of sparkling lights. My eyes were filled with light. There was no darkness! I gazed at the infinite space and declared to the Universe, *"I have come a long way. I have learned much. Yet, in front of the rising Sun I feel naked and acknowledge that*

I know nothing." In this stance of complete surrender of my ego, I felt an incredible sense of freedom. I turned my head to see the shadow of my cross behind me on the sand. I felt like I came out of my cross. I was free at last! Slowly I turned and my eyes followed the golden path of the dawn light to the edge of the horizon. I was standing at the junction between Heaven and Earth. The Sun seemed to be a gateway to the Cosmos. I gazed at it and felt the Presence of the Gatekeeper. With deep reverence, I bowed and said softly, *"I am love."* This was the password that my heart dictated. I expressed the most profound truth in my heart for God is love and the essence of oneness. I entered into silence. In the still moment, I came face to face with my Soul. The quintessential essence touched me and spoke to me of beauty and truth. The attraction was irresistible. I merged as one with the divine essence of my Being. My exalted mind stayed still in silence absorbing the divine vibrations. The aliveness of this mystical experience was a transcendence in which my mind was carried by my Soul to another dimension, a level of ecstatic joy that lies beyond time and space. Suddenly, I was brought back down to this reality by a voice asking me, *"What are you doing?"*

I opened my eyes and saw a woman standing in front of me. I was stunned. Just a few minutes ago, there was no one on the beach. It took me a few seconds to adjust my state of mind. My arms were still outstretched, so I took a deep breath and started to do a downward movement before responding, *"I am doing my exercise."*

She looked puzzled and asked, *"Is this Yoga?"*
"No it is not. It's my own exercise based on the ancient Egyptian Emerald Tablet."

By now, she looked even more puzzled. I showed her the movements and explained the benefits of the exercise. She was satisfied and went on her way. Just before coming on this spiritual retreat, I translated the ancient Egyptian Emerald Tablet knowing that it was an alchemical formula to regenerate body and mind. I converted it into an exercise, a series of gentle movements. I usually do this alignment exercise before meditating.

After this strange encounter, I dove in the ocean and swam in the dawn light. On my way back to the flagpole, I wondered why this woman interrupted my attunement at this precious moment. Was I tested? If so on what? As I was reflecting upon this, the woman returned. She was smiling and said:

"I've done your exercise. Here is a rose for you."
"A rose for me?" I was shocked and asked her, *"Where did you find this rose?"*
"On the beach."

I accepted the rose with gratitude. Somehow, she started to tremble and said that she never comes on the beach so early. I hugged her and said, *"It is ok! One day we will find the purpose of our meeting."* We both knew that we were a part of something greater. We said our farewell and she went on her way. I looked at the red rose and smiled because not only was it the symbol of love and of the Soul, but it was also the emblem of my mystical school. Did I pass an initiation? I began to record this happening in my journal when I realized that I did not know her name. It was important because I could decode it and get some clues to why we met and what was the initiatory test. She was already far away. I ran after her and asked for her name.

"Kathy with a K," she responded.
"Kathy, remember that today is the Egyptian New Year."

We both had big smiles on our faces that revealed our recognition and sympathy as spiritual beings. I walked back to the flagpole still wondering why she interrupted me at this precious moment. What was the initiatory test? I remembered that I had just proclaimed, "I am love" to the Universe. Love! That was it! I had been tested on my understanding of love and how it operates.

When Kathy asked me what I was doing I could have easily said, "Excuse me, I came from far for this special moment. You are interfering with my meditation. Could you please move away?" Luckily, I did not say that as it would have been egotistical. When we meet someone unexpectedly on our spiritual path, our Souls work synergistically for mutual benefit. Indeed, I had been tested on my tolerance, patience, humility, understanding of love and my ability to act in service under any condition of life. How can I seek God in the Universe, if I cannot recognize and honor God in another human being?

After this mystical experience, I took a break from the beach and went for breakfast at a coffee shop. I thought that I deserved a good café with a croissant. It was only 8:30 in the morning and I felt that I had already lived a full day. In these few hours, I felt that I had changed so much. How could I not? I stood up in front of the rising Sun, came out of my cross, entered into the unknown, met with my destiny, had a challenging yet wonderful interplay with Kathy and then received a red rose.

For the rest of the day, I stayed by myself to cherish and guard the warm feeling of love in my heart. At sunset, I sat on a bench by Lake Worth to enjoy the majestic descent of the Sun that marked the end and the fulfillment of this extraordinary day. I was grateful for all the teachings, love, and joy that this day had brought me. Slowly, the Sun disappeared below the horizon and the night began again. I strolled back to my hotel through the beautiful streets of this amazing little town. Along the way, I pondered upon day and night, light and darkness. Ancient Wisdom asserts that darkness is merely the absence of light. I stopped and wrote a note in my journal, "The rising of the

Sun on the horizon symbolizes a passage from the darkness of ignorance into the light of understanding and freedom."

Before going to bed, I studied the symbols that had come to me. I began with number 33 because it all started at 3:30 am when I heard my name called. I used the Baconian Keyboard and after crisscrossing the letters and numbers, I gained more clues that helped me come to a conclusion. I found that number 33 was the equivalence of the word 'free.' The numerical value of the name 'Kathy' was 61, after reflection I saw that this number was linked with two words, love and mercy. I continued further in decoding the name 'Kathy' and discovered within it a hidden signature, 'Your Soul.' It was awe-inspiring. Here was a confirmation of who had called me that morning and who was love and mercy.

The red rose I received from Kathy was a sign that I had passed an initiation that took me beyond the borderline of a limited existence into the infinite realm of the Soul. It was comforting to see that my Soul was lovingly waiting for my coming at the meeting point between Heaven and Earth. I was moved and wrote in my journal, "Today, I responded to the call of my Soul and was touched by my inner beauty and truth. I felt in love with Life itself. The beach was the perfect stage for my rendez-vous with destiny."

With a longing feeling in my heart, I placed the red rose in a crystal vase by my bed. I prayed and fell asleep wondering what tomorrow would bring.

* * *

I began the morning by diving in the ocean. What a way to start the day! Everything was so serene. I floated in the dawn light and became less aware of the water and more aware of the golden light infusing my whole being. Have I become an alchemist? Truly, Nature is the Alchemist 'par excellence.'

In preparing myself for a mystical experience, I drew a circle on the sand and stood in its center. Facing the Sun I asked, *"Is there a magic key to unlock the mysteries of Heaven and Earth?"* Somehow, as if a veil had been lifted from my eyes, I saw for the first time that the Sun above the horizon and its reflecting dawn light on the ocean gave allusion to a natural gigantic ankh. What revelation! I rushed to pick up an ankh that I had in my beach bag. I superimposed it over the image and saw that it was a perfect fit. Nature had revealed once more a symbol of truth.

Key of Life

I recalled that in ancient Egypt, the Ankh was known as the Key of Life. So, I pointed the base of the Ankh toward the Sun as if it were a door with a keyhole, and turned the key. *"This is the magic key. It is the key to unlock the mysteries of Heaven and Earth!"* I exclaimed. I realized that I had in my hand a powerful symbol. Had the ancient Egyptian mystics on their quest for Eternity used the Ankh, and if so how? Three clues came to my mind again: 'image', 'alignment', and 'universal time clock.'

I stepped back into the circle I had drawn on the sand. Facing the eastern horizon, I saw that my circle was within the circle of Earth's horizon, which in turn was within the solar system, the galaxy, and the Universe, circles within circles. Everything was interconnected, interwoven.

From my position, I could see the unity of the Universe and my place in it. As a sign of recognition, I outstretched my arms. *"I'm an ankh too!* I exclaimed. I saw myself as the embodiment of this universal symbol. Here, was the 'image' the first of the three clues. In human terms, the 'image' related to a state of at-one-ment. The second clue, the 'alignment' referred to the rising Sun; and the third clue, the 'universal time clock' related to the celestial timing of the Zodiac.

In the Egyptian Mysteries Schools, when an initiate arrived at the 4th initiation, the heart, he or she emerged into higher life and consciousness, and became an adept. When the adept experienced a moment of Cosmic Harmony or a timeless moment with Eternity, he or she had attained the 7th and final initiation and was given the Ankh or Key of Life as a symbol of fulfillment and illumination. That was the purpose and significance of the Ankh in ancient times.

The seven major levels of initiations and consciousness all link and operate through what is called the Chakra system. There are various symbols given to these levels, which can help us to remember and relate to the levels of consciousness and the process at work. (See page 96)

After my self-realization, I felt a warm feeling of love in my heart. My aura was pulsing with love and light. I saw rainbow arcs of different colors in my aura. *"I radiate what I am."* I said to the Universe. In this expansive state, the world was beautiful, joyful, and golden. There were no needs, no wants, no limitations, and no impossibilities.

I was still in my circle. I closed my eyes and entered into silence. When I opened my eyes, all I could see was the radiance of the Sun before me. I felt a strong attraction and affinity. I extended my hand to reach out. It seemed that the Sun lay tenderly in my hand. For a moment, I beheld the light of my Soul. For a moment, I beheld love, beauty, and truth.

Soul of Light

The attraction and affinity that I felt toward the Sun was due to my recognition that the nature of the Sun, which is fire and light was similar to the nature of my Soul. The English word 'Soul' comes from the Latin word 'Sol' meaning Sun.

Three thousand three hundred years ago, Pharaoh Akhenaton had the same self-realization. He expressed it in his hymns to the Aton, the One God, when he proclaimed, *"Thou art in my heart."* Akhenaton wrote only one prayer to express his love and devotion to God.

> *"I breathe the sweet breath which comes forth from thy mouth.*
> *I behold thy beauty every day.*
> *It is my desire that I may hear thy sweet voice even in the north wind,*
> *That my limbs may be rejuvenated with life through love of thee.*
> *Give me thy hands holding thy Spirit that I may receive it and live by it.*
> *Call thou upon my name unto eternity and it shall never fail."*

Many centuries later, Plotinus, Greek philosopher, shared the same self-realization when he said poetically:

> *"No eye ever saw the Sun without becoming sun like,*
> *Nor can a Soul see beauty without becoming beautiful.*
> *You must become first of all godlike and beautiful*
> *If you intend to see God and beauty."*

That was an ancient way to say that God who is boundless, infinite and eternal does not unite with a human mind that is egocentric, bounded, and limited. God, the Universal Soul, is attracted only to that which is like itself and only unites with the human Soul that is also boundless, infinite, and eternal.

To conclude my mystical experience of that morning, I looked at the Sun and recited the prayer of Akhenaton. I animated it with gestures to amplify the words and play my part as an actor on the stage of the world. I felt like I was romancing Spirit. My aura was so intensified that I could touch it. After the beach, I walked back to my hotel. What a morning I had! But, it was not over yet. As I walked in the lobby, I met a friend who was himself on his spiritual path. We sat in the lobby and exchanged stories and marvels we encountered on our quest. Suddenly, a colorless, condensed flow of energy, like a laser beam of light, burst out of my heart and went straight in his heart. We looked at each other stunned.

"What is this?" He asked.
"Don't move." I replied.

I was unable to say another word. I could not reassure him as I was completely mesmerized by what was happening. I knew that we should never interrupt a creative flow of energy when it manifests itself. We were merely receptive instruments and observers in this outpouring flow of energy. My right cheek and part of my lips became frozen like a dental freeze. I do not know how long we stayed like this maybe a few minutes in linear time, but for us it was a timeless moment. Luckily, there was no one in the lobby. Slowly the beam of energy became weaker and disappeared. When it let us go, we both said at the same time, *"Wow!"* I saw in his eyes that he was shocked and looking at me for an explanation.

"What was that?" He asked again.
"Cosmic Power." I responded.

I explained that Cosmic Power is the creative life force of the Universe that passes through us. The Power is in us but not of us.

"What did you learn from this experience?" I asked him.
"That it flows from heart to heart." He paused for a moment and added, *"To take my spirituality more seriously."*
"What were you practicing this morning?"
"Thai-Chi." He answered.

No wonder! His aura was strong. Just before we met, I was on the beach beholding the Sun and romancing Spirit. When an archetypal energy is accumulated and intensified within us, it must necessarily manifest in our outer reality. It was a visible appearance of the normally invisible energy. Cosmic Power within us sought to find expression and fulfillment as soon as it found an appropriate condition. This mystical experience was for both of us an initiation and a revelation.

We said our good byes and smiled in appreciation for this experience and our sympathy as spiritual beings. On his way out, he said aloud, *"In 40 years, I will never forget it."* He walked away shaking his head. He gave me number 40. It was a clue to discover the meaning and significance of this mystical experience. Number 40 is simply 4 x 10. Number 4 refers to the 4 elements and the 4 cardinal points; hence it is a symbol of foundation, stability and orientation. Number 10 refers to perfection and the return to one. It also indicates a new beginning. Throughout the centuries, prophets and philosophers used number 40 to indicate the completion of purification on four levels: physical, mental, emotional, and spiritual. One was required to be sufficiently pure of body and mind before allowed to enter into the Greater Mysteries of life. On the Chakra system the 4th chakra, the heart, marks this entrance.

Once Cosmic Power has been experienced in one way or another we are never the same again. We can no longer be impressed by the petty powers and successes of the mundane world, which become ridiculous to us. People need to realize and accept the fact that the world is not governed by man-made laws but by universal laws. If we but love God with all our heart and mind, we would be able to discern in our daily life the actuality of Divinity in the midst of myriad illusions of our realities. Our love of truth attracts truth to us, lifts us up so that even in the turbulent world and egocentric strife, we can live on a higher level of consciousness.

This mystical experience increased my understanding about Cosmic Harmony and Power. I realized how important it is for us to create greater harmony and peace in our lives, because the law of Karma or Compensation is at work at all times; cause and effect are never separated. I realized how important it is to trust and follow the guidance of our Soul pointing the way to enlightenment. I realized how precious life is and what a miraculous gift life is for humanity.

After this encounter, I went back to my room to take notes. For the rest of the day, I stayed by myself cherishing this energy in my heart.

* * *

The next morning, I arrived on the beach at sunrise. It was my third and last day of my retreat; my plane was scheduled to leave in the afternoon. That morning I sat on a rock staring at the ocean. With the coming and going of the waves, the ocean was telling me that there is a time to come and a time to go. I felt sad as my heart was longing for more mystical experiences. The beach had been an open University for education of my mind and stimulation of my Soul's consciousness.

I gazed at the ocean and saw sparkling lights dancing on the ocean forming a line. I took my camera and went closer. I extended my hand to reach out and touch the mystery of light. The connection was gentle as I felt the energy going throughout my body. The coming together of two opposite polarities, light and matter, ethereal and concrete, was harmonious creating a symphony of sound and light. *"It all starts in light and ends in light."* I murmured.

Light & Matter

The play of light mirrored on the ocean revealed a profound truth about actuality, reality, and destiny. I saw that the letter Z was taking form. I looked at it without thinking to allow the experience of connectedness to run its course. I felt mesmerized. It was another experience with Cosmic Power. I stayed with the energy until it dissipated. When it let me go, I dove in the ocean to bathe in that light. Back on the rock, I reflected on the letter Z, another clue for me to decode. As the last letter of the alphabet, it indicated the omega point, the end of something; hence, it denoted the end and fulfillment of my retreat. On the highest spiritual level, the letter Z indicated the Greek God Zeus, known as the Father of Light. In Christianity, it refers to the Christ Spirit. The radiance of the Light of God is Love. Love is Light and Life.

I was deep into my thoughts when a breaking wave splashed me and reminded me that it was time to go. I closed my retreat with gratitude for the unforgettable mystical experiences I had the privilege to live and enjoy. That morning I brought a rose with me to throw in the ocean as a farewell gesture.

Rose in Sands of Time

Before I did this, I took a picture and named it, 'Rose in Sands of Time' because it represented the incarnation of my Soul in this lifetime, and my rendez-vous with destiny. Just before throwing the rose in the ocean, I kissed it and promised to come back to celebrate Universal Life.

I had a little more time so I went for a jog along the beach. I felt a sense of freedom and accomplishment. Suddenly, I heard a little voice behind me shouting, *"God bless you. God bless you."* I stopped and turned around. On the top of a sand dune a women came running toward me and said enthusiastically, *"I appreciate what you are doing."*

I was not sure what she was referring to so I asked her; "What do you think I am doing?
"I think that you sent good energy to the world, to clear the Earth."
"Yes, I did." In fact, when I closed my retreat, I did some movements to ground the energy. I asked her if she would like to redo them with me.

Her face lit up. *"Last week, I asked God to put me in touch with the right person for a spiritual retreat,"* she said.
"What's your name?" I asked.
"Rosa."
"What a nice name!"

Here is another rose! I thought inwardly. When we finished the exercise, we conversed a little more. I invited her to join me on my next retreat. She was so happy. We hugged and said our farewell. As I walked away, she said again, *"God bless you."* I was moved by her blessings.

In the plane, I recorded my mystical experiences of the day. I finished with the name Rosa. The rose is an ancient mystical symbol of love, idealism, nobility, and the unfolding beauty of the Soul. I recalled that Jesus was known as the Rose of Sharon. I used the Baconian Keyboard to get more insights; the total numeric value of the name 'Rosa' was 50. This number is also the numeric value of the word 'love.' What a wonderful symbol of truth she was!

Then, my thoughts went to my Egyptian guide, the illustration of a mystic lady who had inspired me to come on this retreat. I appreciated the simplicity and universality of her gesture and sense of identification. I felt the divine Love she felt; I discovered the stars that she had followed thousands of years ago and became aware of their significance. To understand her, I had to keep in mind that she lived in a world of symbolic images and myths that reflected Heaven, Earth, Creation, the beginning of Time, and that she was on her quest for Eternity. I was certain that she must have been a graduate of the Mystery Schools of Initiation in which a student was given a series of progressive teachings and experiences that affected them physically, psychologically, and spiritually. Once a student had reached a sufficient purity of mind and body, he or she became an initiate. In this state of being, the initiate entered into a higher life and consciousness, and was allowed to evoke a moment of Cosmic Harmony, thus with Eternity.

Each year, I returned to Palm Beach for a summer retreat to celebrate the Egyptian New Year and Universal Life. Each time the Spirit of Nature welcomed me and my Soul waited for my coming at the threshold between Heaven and Earth. Each time it was a moving experience. On the beach, I continued to participate in the universal interplay taking pictures and following the guidance of my Soul that led to ever-greater discoveries. The symbols and clues followed in sequence and each contributed to the unfoldment of my consciousness and future stages of development. My participation in the Universal Life and interplay became a way of life, a continuous adventure with all the excitements and treasures I could ever ask for on my journey into oneness.

Chapter 2

Universal Life & Interplay

*"One cannot help but be in awe
When one contemplates the mysteries of eternity, of life,
Of the marvelous structure of reality."*

~Albert Einstein

We are living in the midst of invisible and visible worlds. In this chapter, I will share some mystical photographs I took throughout the years while on my spiritual retreats in Palm Beach. Some images were concrete while others were subtle and ethereal. Some were visible on Earth while others in the sky. All conveyed succinct messages and profound teachings. Our Soul and the Soul of the Universe can express themselves in a lovely and dynamic way, and what a better place than in the midst of Nature, the infinite source of correspondences.

As I continued on my spiritual path, the use of symbolic thinking became essential. It was an art of thinking in images instead of words. It opened up a channel of communication between my mind and Soul. The Soul used symbolic images and synchronicities to communicate a teaching, gave a confirmation and offered encouragement to guide my next step. When a symbolic image appears spontaneously in our mind or a living symbol 'pops' suddenly in front of us out of nowhere, the purpose is to awaken and arouse our heightened consciousness so that we may join our inner and outer worlds, the spiritual with material, the invisible with visible.

The Crowned Ibis

After meditation and exercises on the beach, I rode my bicycle along the golf course toward the famous Breakers Hotel to pick up an information package. From afar, I saw a pond of lotus flowers. "Here is a perfect image of the alchemical process at work," I thought. I stopped to take a picture of this beautiful scenery, when suddenly a white bird came out of nowhere and stood on a lotus leaf. It definitely wanted to be in the picture too!

The Crowned Ibis

In Alchemy, the lotus flower is often taken as a symbol of the higher mental consciousness opening to the Sun or Soul. This symbol relates to the elements and helps us remember the different levels of the consciousness. It describes the process the human consciousness must undergo in order to reach enlightenment and then spiritual illumination.

The muddy earth, out of which the lotus flower grows, represents the physical and mundane world in which we live. The lotus stem grows up through the water of the astral level, (the lower self of the human psyche or personality), and brings out its leaves; and then, produces its flower in the air of the mental level. As the flower opens, it reveals its pure heart with the sparkling jewel, 'the jewel in the lotus.' The flame of the heart represents this jewel. Both relate to the fifth element or the quintessence, the essence and beauty of the Soul. This is the level of the heart and of spiritual consciousness.

Purity of Mind
The white lotus flowers and the whiteness of the bird emphasized the purity of the mind. We cannot search for knowledge and truth without having a certain degree of purity of mind and body. To reach a sufficient purity of mind, we need to control our ego, our lower self, its emotions, desires and thoughts, which can be selfish, possessive, obsessive, and easily disturbed and troubled. We also need to become more aware of ourselves and reclaim our projections on things and people, since all ego identifications are projections and illusions. On the body level, we need to control the physical appetites, food, alcohol, drugs, and sexuality. It is only through the development of self-love, self-respect, discipline, will power and the right effort that we can overcome the abuses and illusions of our own or someone else's egocentric mind.

Mind and Soul
For mind and Soul to connect and work together, first we must surrender the ego to have peace of mind. There must be clarity of mind capable of clear perception and free of dogmatic theories. To reflect

accurately the light of the Soul, the mind has to be kept clear like a crystal or a clear polished mirror. It requires that we become aware of the quality of our love and intentions in whatever we do and with whomever we are with at anytime. Emotional love of the lower self should not be confused with that of pure heart love. First, we must have a sufficient purity of mind in order to love truly from the heart in a balanced, peaceful, unpossessive, and unselfish way. When we are able to do this, the heart opens like a beautiful flower pulsing with love. At this level, we emerge into a higher level of consciousness.

The white ibis bird represented the air element, which is associated with purity of mind, harmony of thoughts and enlightenment. In ancient Egypt, the ibis bird was the emblem of Thoth, the great scribe, teacher, and messenger of God. I was amazed and amused to see on the picture that a purplish lotus flower crowned the head of the bird. The color purple is related to the 7th chakra, the crown, and the 7th initiation symbolizing divinity, royalty, wisdom, joy and illumination. A state of illumination is the union with Christ's Spirit achieved through divine Love; there are many degrees of illumination, the first one begins at the 4th initiation.

How did the bird happen to be at the right place and the right time? What were the underlying cosmic forces? As an observer, when I saw the bird coming out of nowhere to position himself a on a lotus leaf, I recognized that it was an interaction of my Soul with the Spirit of Nature to create the synchronicity that would give a complete image of the fourth and fifth element. This imagery was created for the purpose of teaching, revelation, and enjoyment.

After taking notes, I continued riding toward the Breakers Hotel. Along the way, I was surprised to see a hotel plaque with number 330 with four large balls beside it, two white and two red. The plaque revealed the signature of the author behind this interplay. In the previous chapter we saw that the number 33 related to the word 'free' and that the equivalent of number 3 was the letter 'C', therefore 33 can become 'CC' which is a code for Christ or Cosmic Consciousness. The zero either indicates the 'One and All' or null, nothing at all. The color red and white of the balls represented Spirit and Soul. What a wonderful confirmation.

Arriving at the grand entrance of the hotel, I looked around for a bicycle stand. There was none. A valet parking attendant asked me to leave my bicycle with him. I was surprised. I could not believe that my bike could be valet parked! I went inside to pick up the package at the receptionist's desk; when I came out of the hotel, I called the attendant to bring back my bicycle. While I was waiting, a big black limousine pulled up in front of me. The chauffeur hurried to open the door. And here, I met another kind of reality.

A tall slim man in a three piece-suit, nice tie, black glasses, and a cell phone in his hand came out of the limousine and stood beside me while typing a text message. As I waited silently for my bicycle, I felt somewhat awkward as I was casually dressed in shorts, T-shirt, and flip-flops with no make-up. These few minutes were for me a very long time. At last, the attendant came back with my bicycle. I told him that as I had just come from the beach and did not have any money to tip him. He smiled and said kindly, *"Don't worry about it."* Meanwhile, the distinguished guest finished texting, and started to talk aloud on the phone walking his way into the hotel lobby with a proud attitude completely ignoring his surroundings. I saw the humor in the juxtaposition of our realities. I rode away between the majestic rows of tall palm trees appreciating my reality and continued with my day.

To project a proud attitude and an assumed confidence is to fool ourselves. Such attitude reveals our insecurity and level of consciousness. People whose purpose in life is to make money, achieve fame and power are like the living dead; they live in the illusions of their deceived, egocentric mind. When Jesus talked about the dead, he was referring to people who were physically alive, but were like living dead because they were ignorant and unaware to any kind of spiritual life. All of us are partly dead and partly living. That is why it is so important to work daily on our spirituality. Life provides the conditions and opportunities we need for our spiritual awakening. Once a person is awakened by the Spirit, he or she becomes alive, becomes raised in consciousness and makes the effort to live truly. The mere fact of living and evolving is a privilege.

The Power of Money
Money is powerful because not only can it buy things, but also because it is a man-made energy. As energy, it has polarities and needs to flow. With an attitude of 'non-attachment' toward money, we allow it to flow back and forth between two poles. When the flow of energy returns, it comes back with multiplied effects or blessings. It is our attitude towards money that creates either prosperity or suffering and struggles. The way we give is the way we shall receive. Money is not the root of our problems, but rather it is our attitude of greediness and manipulation that cuts us off from the return flow of money blessings. Sometimes money comes our way and then is taken away for a very good reason. It teaches us about our character and karmic lessons we have yet to cancel. There is nothing wrong with material success and prosperity. Prosperity has many definitions; we may define it as health, happiness, and financial security. It is difficult to enjoy life and be on our spiritual path when we are hungry and financially insecure. It would be more productive and enjoyable if we could create a comfortable and beautiful environment.

The secret of lasting success in all things lies in genuine self-confidence, not an assumed confidence, blind faith, or mere belief. An assumed confidence needs external support and approval from the mundane world, while a genuine confidence gives support. The word 'confidence' is made up of the Latin prefix 'con' meaning 'with' and 'fidere' meaning 'to trust.' A genuine confidence is an intense trust in the guidance of the Soul. Our own Soul is our best friend, advisor, healer, comforter, and inner teacher whom we can truly trust because our Soul knows where we have been, where we are, and where we are going.

Once true self-confidence is achieved, we find that we can be open to life, give support, and share our joy and knowledge with others so that they too can experience their own Soul. This state of being is often accompanied by qualities and experiences of oneness, humility, gratitude, creativity, enthusiasm, contentment, kindness, joy, and inner peace.

* * *

Creative Power

Ancient philosophers, poets, artists, and inventors symbolized the source of their ideas as a goddess or muse who inspired and presided over their creative arts. The source of their inspiration came really from their own Soul, God within. In the creative process, the mind uses both sides of the brain in order to release inner knowledge and power. The process involves focused attention on both sides, the right side, an active 'doing' and the left side, a passive yet receptive 'not doing.' The active 'doing' part requires study, concentration, and analysis. The passive 'non-doing' involves relaxing the mind so that it may be receptive to insight, intuition, and inspiration.

After my meditation and exercises on the beach, I sat under my umbrella enjoying the present moment and reflected upon the creative process of 'doing' and 'not-doing.' I wondered if I was doing both at the same time. I saw some birds walking along the beach. To my surprise one of them found its nesting place in my footprint it was definitely resting and 'not- doing' anything at all. Two other birds kept walking, hence 'doing.' I was amused to see a little bird, a little further away, standing by overlooking the scene and also wondering what this 'doing' and 'not-doing' was all about. All birds, from the black sparrow to the white dove, signify thoughts in symbology.

Birds Interplay

I realized that I had in front of me a living symbolic image of the creative process. This living image was due to an interaction of my Soul with the Spirit of Nature for the purpose of teaching, revelation, and enjoyment.

Upon reflection, I realized that it emphasized that the 'doing' was as important as the 'not-doing.' Every active stage must be balanced by a passive stage, so that the two modes of the brain can function in a complementary and dynamic way to produce and manifest a creative work. Therefore, focus of attention on both sides of the brain is essential to manifest our creative power.

In 1687, when Sir Isaac Newton, mathematician and Rosicrucian, took a break from his research, he sat under a tree to relax and appreciate Nature. While relaxing he discovered the law of Gravity when an apple fell from a tree. How did this coincidence happen? During the relaxing stage of the creative process, there is a let go that allowed his thoughts to shift and realign themselves. At the same time, he balanced and harmonized the left and right side of the brain. By doing so, he allowed the Soul to interact with his environment and assist in the discovery. When he saw the apple falling, he suddenly realized how the natural phenomenon of gravity worked. That was a moment of illumination, which is in itself a mystical experience.

The same method of creativity can be applied when we are faced with life's challenges; we can relax the objective mind and release our problems to the power of the Soul. In this way, we can stand up for ourselves and resolve our problems in a peaceful way. The more we can understand and apply the art and science of creative thinking, the more we will be able to release our creative power.

Leaving the beach, I saw a man doing some kind of Yoga exercise; his hands were joined together over his head and he was trying hard to keep his balance on one leg. I stopped and said jokingly, *"You need two legs to go through life!"* He laughed and came toward me to introduce himself. We talked about different types of eastern and western exercises. I mentioned that I designed my own exercise by decoding the Emerald Tablet of the ancient Egyptians. He understood the alchemical process and asked me to show him the movements. We did the exercise together. When we finished I brought to his attention a truck passing by on which was written, "Boost Way." We laughed aloud.

"Here is your message of the day!" I exclaimed.
"So true! That's what I needed," he replied.

He was grateful for the sharing and amazed on how the universal interplay works. We said our farewell and he went on his way.

* * *

The Awakening Angel

Often on my retreats, I would encounter strange imagery in the sky. One morning as I strolled along the beach towards my flagpole's alignment, in the dark clouds I saw a face looking down on the ocean with rays of light streaming out of an open mouth. I recognized that it was a creational myth. It reminded me of a biblical quote, *"And the spirit of God moved upon the face of the waters."* I stopped to appreciate the scenery and took a picture. As I looked higher in the sky, I saw in the white clouds a silhouette of a running angel sounding a trumpet with a banner hanging off the instrument. I did not hear the sounds of the trumpet, but I realized that what I was seeing was a thought-form of God stamped in the clouds. The word 'angel' means 'divine idea' or 'thought-form of God.'

The Awakening Angel

The whole image seemed to relate to Creation, Time, and Humanity. Was it a confirmation for the global awakening we are experiencing? Arriving at my flagpole's alignment, I opened up my arms and began to do the 'Emerald Tablet Exercise.' A woman and a little girl stopped by and asked if they could join me. I explained the movements and we started to do the exercise together. I looked at the little girl and told her, *"You're doing good."* When we finished the exercise, she came to me and said:
"I always make mistake between good and God."

I looked into her blue eyes and replied, *"It is not a mistake because God is good."*

She gave me a big smile. I caressed her blond hair and said that she looked like a little angel and asked for her name. With a sweet little voice she responded, *"Isabelle."*

"You are Isis the beautiful!" I exclaimed.

Her whole face radiated with happiness. She asked who Isis was. So, I explained that Isis was an ancient Egyptian goddess like the Virgin Mary. The lady who accompanied Isabelle smiled and was grateful for the sharing. As they went on their way, the little girl kept turning back waving good-bye with a big smile. I was happy about the connection. I sent her a good-bye kiss. Each time we connect with the Soul of another person, young or old, the experience is a timeless moment. Isabelle was a little angelic messenger who gave me two clues, 'Good' and 'God.' For me that was a confirmation of who was behind the image in the sky and our meeting.

The word God is an English name used commonly to define the Absolute Being, the All-Goodness. Hence, whatever we do that is good, just and unselfish is then in accordance with the Will of God, the Will of Love.

* * *

Rainbow Around the Sun

During one of my summer retreats, I went back to the beach in the afternoon. Just as I entered the beach, I was amazed to see a full circle rainbow around the Sun. I was so excited. I rushed to draw a circle on the sand in imitation of the rainbow and said aloud, *"As above, so below."* I lay down in the circle to have a larger view and took a dozen pictures. I then attuned myself with this archetype to tap in its vital energy and join with Universal Life.

Rainbow Around the Sun

A full rainbow circle is rare. The Sun and the raindrops have to be in just the right place at the right time. And so was I to witness such a beautiful symbol. It provides insight into the creational alchemy of life and the nature of the human Soul. The Sun, as the central dot, represents the element of fire, the life force, and life giving of Spirit. The rainbow's circle represents the Soul, the life form and the element of water. Spirit dwells within the Soul. They complement each other and are one. Thus, the rainbow around the Sun is a universal symbol of harmony and oneness and a signature of the One God.

A circle with a central dot is one of the most fundamental symbols of life itself. It is the symbol of conception, the egg and sperm. It also symbolizes the Sun, the alchemical Gold, the Alpha and Omega, Creation and Evolution. In ancient Egypt, it was the symbol of number 1, the beginning of all things and measurement.

In Christianity, the rainbow has always been the universal symbol of the Ark of the Covenant between Heaven and Earth. The covenant has to do with loving God with all one's heart, mind, and strength, and to love one another with a pure heart.

The appearance of a rainbow around the Sun was for me a sign of hope and a strong cosmic message. At that time, summer 2001, we were experiencing violent world events. So, I took it as a message that humanity needs to live in harmony and peace in order to fulfill its destiny.

Since the beginning of 2000, the new millennium, we have had several violent events around the world. On the morning of September 11, 2001, I was studying ancient Wisdom when I received an intuitive message saying, *"Behold Good."* I was puzzled because I was meditating and studying at that time. I wondered for whom that message was intended. I reflected upon these two words. The word 'behold' means to hold or to see. The word good is synonymous to God. To see also means to understand. So, I concluded that the Universe was reminding us to have good, positive thoughts and actions. I had no sooner finished this translation when I received a phone call urging me to turn on the television to watch the horrible attack on the Trade Center Towers in New York. I was shocked and cried. What a tragedy for humanity. I immediately prayed for the Souls of the people killed, their family, the country, and humanity.

While watching the event on television, in the dark clouds surrounding the falling towers I saw the face of evil. *"But evil exists only in the mind of mankind."* I said with a heavy heart. What I saw was an evil thought-form stamped in the dark clouds. The message

"Behold Good" I received that morning was making more sense now. It was a warning for humanity about the possibility of self-destruction. When we are cut off or out of tune with the universal creative flow of life, we suffer the consequences on personal, national, and global levels. Earth, a little blue dot in the Cosmos, will go on its course for millions of years with us or without us.

Although there were constant threats from terrorists and red and yellow warning flags for traveling I decided to go to Palm Beach for my winter retreat, which I called 'Tending the Flame.' I recalled when Jesus said that at the end of the Age, in which we are right now, there would be wars but not to be afraid. So, I refused to live in fear as the fanatic terrorists wanted us to. Instead, I chose to celebrate life. I knew that I had to be careful but also that I must dare to take up challenges and move on unafraid. There were only three people in the plane and my hotel was empty, but I was happy that I made the decision to go on my retreat.

Evil is darkness at work; it feeds on fear, confusion and corruption. It feeds on its self. Unfortunately, some media and 'so-called' charities helped in the feeding. Let us remember, at all times, that there are millions of good and sincere people doing their best to create a better world. Let us give them our support and encouragement.

As I reflected upon this past decade, the relationship between the terrorist attacks of 2001 and the economic crisis of 2008 was definitely due to man-made madness. The madness of an egocentric mind is the result of evil, ignorance, selfishness, stupidity, vanity, arrogance, and greed. Evil is the work of the egocentric mind of an individual and groups of like-minded people.

In Christianity, Satan represents evil. After being challenged by Satan, Jesus said, *"Get thee behind me, Satan. Thou art an offence unto me, for thou savourest not the things that be of God, but those that be of men."* Note well that Jesus gave a direct order, 'Get thee behind me.' He did not say walk with me. It could not be because we cannot be 'in light' and 'in darkness' at the same time. It is one or the other. This statement indicates a different level of consciousness. In the Chakra system, Jesus represents the heart chakra. Satan represents the negative aspect of our lower chakras and the egocentric mind.

We empower ourselves knowing that Satan, as the tempter and challenger, represents our own testing faculty that constantly tests us on our sincerity, strength, courage, and humility. Our own ego can close our eyes and ears and can even cause us to run away and deny the very same light we search for in our lives. We can be our own best friend or worst enemy.

Shakespeare said it succinctly, *"To be or not to be, that is the question."* It is a choice of consciousness between light and darkness that we have to make at all times. If we encourage darkness to spread in any way, consciously or unconsciously, we are as guilty as those who have created it. Let us remember that the universal Justice of the law of Karma is at work at all times, *"As we sow, so will we reap."* The energies set in motion are retributive in nature; they follow the fundamental principles of cause and effect. In order to remove the effect, we need first remove the cause.

Let us 'Behold Good' and work on cancelling our own negative karma to free ourselves. Let each one of us begin with self-regeneration before dreaming of a social and global one.

* * *

The Mystical Leonardo da Vinci

In the spring 2010, I was fortunate to be in Los Angeles when the famous Getty Museum had an exhibition on Leonardo da Vinci. With a quiet excitement, I strolled through this remarkable exposition enjoying every moment of it. I ended up at the gift shop where I noticed that the Vitruvian Man illustration was on the cover of some notebooks. As I reached to pick up the last small notebook, from the corner of my eye I saw a hand rushing to pick it up. Unfortunately for this person I was fast enough to secure it. We then looked at each other and laughed.

"I wish that they would have shown the mystical Leonardo da Vinci." I said.
"Me too!" She responded.

She introduced herself as Elba. Right away, I recognized the symbolic meaning of her name. I knew that our meeting was an important synchronicity. We shared our appreciation for the exhibition and our admiration for the genius of Leonardo da Vinci. Before leaving, she gave me a business card and we said our farewell. I went outside on a terrace overlooking the mountains of Malibu and the Pacific Ocean. I sat on a bench for a peaceful moment enjoying this beautiful panorama. I had her card in my hand. It was a white card with a striking royal blue shield with three golden Fleur de Lys stamped on it. 'A sign of royalty,' I thought. Kings and Queens applied the Fleur de Lys on their crown, so it became an emblem of royalty. That is why the Fleur de Lys is also associated with the crown chakra, the shining crown of illumination. The color blue of the shield indicated the celestial realm of the Soul. The color gold of the flowers indicated the Spirit. As I pondered upon these clues, suddenly I remembered another significant synchronicity I had, years ago, when the Fleur de Lys came to me in a strange way.

It was in the year 2000, when I was visiting the Rosicrucian bookstore in San Jose, California. A sales clerk asked me if I needed help; I answered that I was just browsing. A few moments later, as I was looking up at books on a higher shelf, a book suddenly came out in a straight line, suspended in air just as if an invisible hand was holding it and then fell right in front of me. The sales clerk and I looked at each other in shock we both had jaws open. I picked up the book and said,

"I guess that I found my book!"
"How could this happen?" she asked me.
"Through the power of my Soul," I replied.
"From time to time, I have seen this happened," she said shaking her head.

It was a big white book, which seemed to be a rare esoteric book. I did not open it on the spot because I felt I needed to be alone in order to discover the subliminal guidance it would give me. When my Soul uses its transcendent powers to guide me, I feel that it is my spiritual duty to research the meaning, purpose, and significance of the guidance.

That evening before opening the book, I asked for guidance and then opened it at random. It fell on a chapter entitled, "Mythic History of the Fleur de Lys." I studied and synthesized all the clues; the message was about the sublime glorification of the Soul. That was the first time the Fleur de Lys came to me so powerfully. When I saw the three golden Fleur de Lys on Elba's card, I knew that I was guided further into its mystery. I decoded the name of Elba and the symbols on her card, all the clues pointed to the way of enlightenment.

The Vitruvian Man brought Elba and I together. So, I thought that it would be through him that I would discover more about the mystical Leonardo da Vinci, and hopefully discover some hidden clues encoded in the illustration. The Vitruvian Man is also known as the Universal Man of Light.

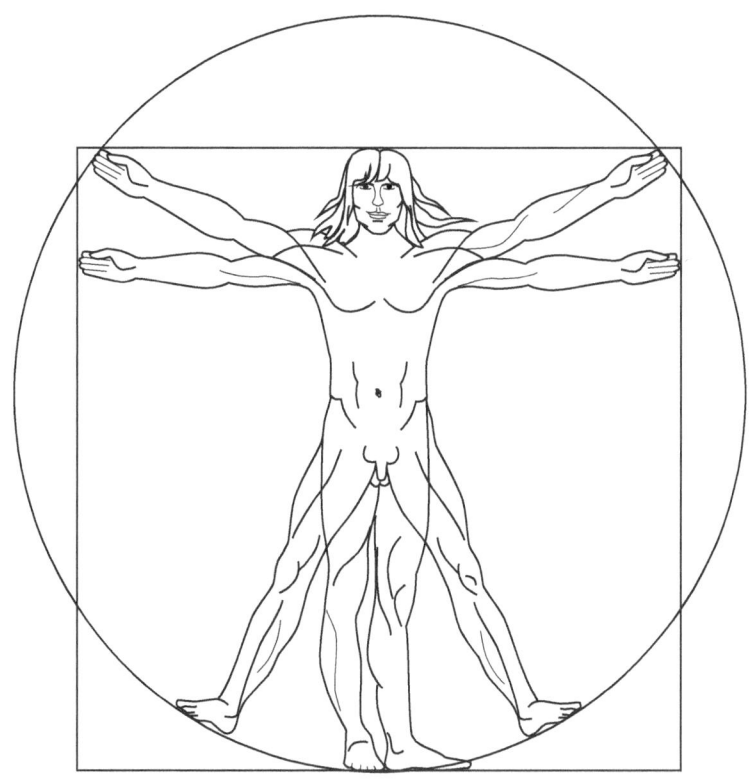

The Universal Man of Light

The Vitruvian Man illustration of Leonardo da Vinci was named after Vitruvius, a Roman architect and engineer. Leonardo da Vinci (1452-1519), a Rosicrucian, incorporated in his works the art and science of metaphysics and mysticism. Many of his inventions in diverse fields of science were not yet possible in his lifetime. Throughout this illustration, Leonardo demonstrated that reality is an inner experience and that the human being is a revelation of truth in geometry and proportion. Leonardo believed that the human body is divine and one of the most beautiful forms of life.

Within this illustration, there are systematic designs to teach and assist us to remember universal laws, so that we may discover profound truths about our own nature, reality, and destiny. Leonardo focuses our attention on the square and the circle, however there are also invisible triangles all encoded with mystical meanings and messages.

Geometry Speaks

The Vitruvian Man's hands and feet touching the square indicate that balance and harmony within and without, are required to achieve self-mastery. Number 4 is associated with stability and wholeness. The square refers to the 4 elements, the 4 seasons and 4 cardinal points. We can see that the genitals mark the center point of the square to indicate the source of creative power that gives and spreads life, the life giving fire. The nudity denotes that one must stand naked or egoless in front of God.

With his hands and feet outstretched and touching the circle, the Vitruvian Man indicates the expansion of the mind into the spiritual world. The circle represents space filled with all potentialities. Here, the navel marks the center point to indicate spiritual rebirth. The space between the outstretched legs reveals an upward triangle, symbolizing the fire element. It indicates that we need to increase our inner fire in order to achieve spiritual rebirth.

To find more invisible triangles and more clues and revelations, we need to draw a circle within the square. The top of the head and the feet touching the square mark the two opposite polarities. From the top of the head, we draw two equal lines downward joined with a third to create an equilateral triangle. Then from the feet, we draw a similar triangle, but this one pointing downward. We can recognize in these two interlaced triangles the six-pointed Star of David symbolizing union of two opposite polarities, male and female, fire and water. It also represents the mystical marriage of mind and Soul. The 7th central point marks the point of balance, harmony, power and manifestation.

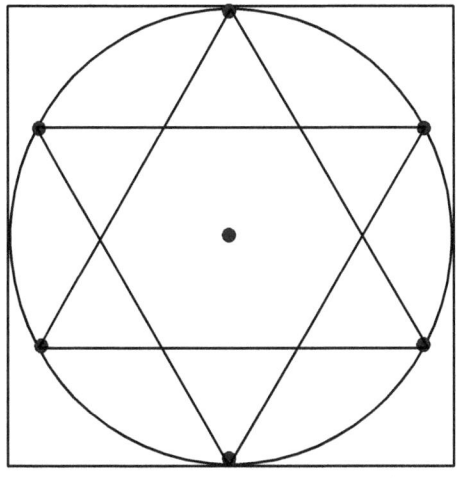

Star of David

From this same six-point symmetry, we can design the Flower of Life with its petals. This pattern reflects the principles of balance, harmony, and beauty. The Flower of Life symbolizes the beauty of life and the blossoming of the creative mind.

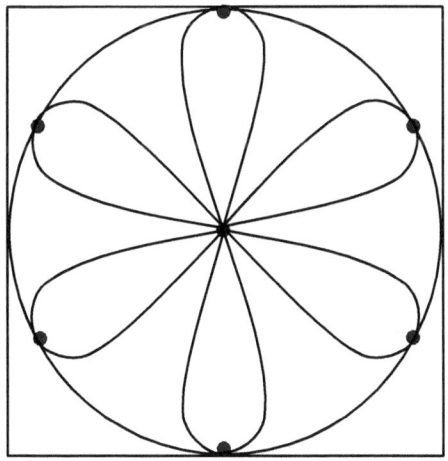

Flower of Life

Other archetypal patterns like the Tree of Life, the Chakras systems can be displayed within this circle.

Numbers Speak

Ancient philosophers and mathematicians believed that life unfolded according to archetypal patterns, images, and numbers. They all used the Golden Ratio or Golden Proportion formula to express universal wisdom about harmony, beauty, and existence.

The Golden Ratio is often presented as an unfolding golden spiral. In Nature, this symmetry can be found in the head of a sunflower, the spiral of a conch or nautilus shell, the curve of a wave and a spiraling galaxy. All demonstrate the order and harmony of the Cosmos and the beauty of life. In the Fibonacci system, the Golden Ratio is represented by a sequence of number relationships: 1, 1, 2, 3, 5, 8, 13, 21, 34, 55, 89, 144, 233 … in which each number is the sum of the two preceding numbers. Whenever we see numbers starting like the Fibonacci series 1,1,2 it usually signals a new beginning of some kind.

The double digital code 11:11 indicates spiritual awakening. When the double digital number increases 22, 33, to 99 it indicates our emergence into spiritual reality and the expansion of consciousness. We can see them on digital clocks, computers, dates, license plates or in other ways. Each number has its own meaning and purpose for us to discover and study. We may find more understanding and guidance through different corresponding systems like the Chakra system, the Tree of Life, the Wheel of Time and Space, the Tarot etc.

As we continue to follow the guidance, it will eventually bring us to the triple digital code 111, 222, 333 to 999 to indicate the expansion of the mind into higher levels of consciousness, in which realities are continually transformed with greater potential for accomplishments. With this awareness we become more universal.

The Vitruvian Man brought Elba and I together. She acted like a messenger when she gave me her card with the striking three golden Fleur de Lys. Each flower had three petals; hence, it denoted the threefold nature of life and the triple digital code 333. Furthermore, the Fleur de Lys geometric form denoted a movement of energy rising upward and then arching down.

I realized that it indicated the rising of the energy from the base of the spine rising upward and then bursting through the head, the crown chakra. This movement of energy shows us how to regenerate ourselves. I was pleased to see that it was similar to my exercise, which is based on the ancient Egyptian Emerald Tablet formula.

What was the connection between the Fleur de Lys and the Vitruvian Man? I wondered. Both spoke of self-mastery and the way to enlightenment. That was the purpose of my synchronicity with Elba, which was guided by my Soul and the Universal Soul wherein are all the invisible Masters.

The Vitruvian Man was really an illustration of the 'Universal Man of Light' an ideal archetype for humanity. Through his encoded guidance, Leonardo aroused our curiosity so that we may discover profound truths about our nature, reality, and destiny.

To pay homage to Leonardo da Vinci and to discover more revelations, I decoded his full name on the Baconian Keyboard. The total numeric value of the name Leonardo da Vinci in the Simple Cipher was 138, and without 'da' it came to 133. These two numbers were significant. I had to look at the meaning of each number individually:

Number 1 indicated the Absolute, the One God.
Number 3 referred to the Holy Trinity.
Number 8 is the numeric symbol of Hermes, Mercury, and the sign of Infinity and Eternity.

888 (three eights) is the mystical number of Jesus Christ. Number 8 is emblematic of Regeneration, Resurrection, Completion, Glory, Perfection, and Paradise regained.

I finished decoding number 138 by looking at the correspondence of numbers with letters. Number 1 is equivalent to letter 'A', which is linked to Creation and the One God. Number 3 is equivalent to the letter 'C' and number 8 to the letter 'H.' The mystical code 'CH' is a cipher for the Christ.

Number 133 indicated the highest degree of initiation and the attainment of self-mastery. The word 'free' equals 33, which is the equivalent of the letters 'CC' meaning Cosmic or Christ Consciousness.

After decoding his full name, I recalled that Leonardo signed his initials as L.V, which totalized 31, three in one, meaning Trinity-in-Unity. I continued by crisscrossing the letters with numbers. I was shocked to see that the word 'love' became apparent and stood out on the keyboard. Was Leonardo da Vinci sending a message of love through time and space?

And so, the Rose of Leonardo da Vinci unfolded during the European Renaissance. Leonardo works revealed profound truths about natural, human, and divine nature, and the destiny of humanity. He was an illuminated human being and one of the great Master Souls.

To research and follow the clues given by our own Soul and the Master Souls is to find oneself on an incredible treasure trail filled with mystical adventures. In the fiction book, 'The Da Vinci Code' the author was inspired by some information concerning genuine secrets about a line of Master Souls. Peter Dawkins, a recognized authority in Western Wisdom Traditions, affirms that there really was a code and also a Grail secret – and still is. Peter informs us that the line of Master Souls from Leonardo da Vinci extends to Francis Bacon and the Comte de Saint Germain. I feel honored and privileged to follow Peter's footsteps. His wonderful work helped me speed up my personal transformation that resulted in the gift of this book.

Chapter 3

The Holographic Universe

One of the most serious challenges we face on our spiritual path is to move on with an intelligent open-mindedness. We must explore the unknown without anxiety, integrate different concepts in our thinking, and rely as much on our intuition as on our intellect so that we may apply the art and science of creative thinking. This is not an easy task, for it requires love, dedication, and trust in the guidance of the Soul.

On my spiritual retreat of 2010 in Palm Beach, I explored further the nature of reality, the holographic Universe, and the Egyptian cosmological mystery. At the beginning of this book, I mentioned that while studying reality I was inspired by an illustration of an Egyptian mystic who stood in front of the rising Sun. This multidimensional image needed no words. The ancient Egyptians knew that symbolic images and action could transmit throughout the millenniums immediate information about the nature of reality and the structure of the Universe.

According to Wisdom Traditions, a human being is a reflection of the Universe and embodies it on every level. Every cell in our body contains the information of the whole Universe like a hologram, in which each part of the hologram contains all the information possessed by the whole; each part is capable of reconstructing the entire hologram. A hologram is a light interference pattern. Modern scientists can create a hologram by splitting a laser light in two and bouncing it off mirrors through microscope lenses. The meeting of the two rays creates an interference pattern on the film, which can be projected as a three-dimensional image in space. If the hologram is cut off in pieces, the entire image can still be projected from each piece but the intensity would be reduced.

The theories and publications of physicist David Bohm explain the nature of the Universe as an enfolding order consisting of a realm of frequencies and potentialities underlying an illusion of concreteness. Modern neuroscientists have discovered analogous mechanism in their studies of the operation of the human mind. It may be that not only the Universe operates like a gigantic hologram but also the human mind. In creating a reality, the mind may operate like a hologram. It's mind blowing!

This incredible theory into the holographic Universe offers us an explanation for the mystical experiences of connectedness, illumination, and transcendence in which there is access to the spiritual realms. It is the mystic who through inner attunement of mind and Soul experiences and interprets the Universal Mind, the infinite expression of the One God.

From my mystical experiences, I realized that my mind acts as a mirror reflecting my inner Light so that I can see it on the screen of my mind or in my environment. It works the same way as the Sun light striking a prism that diffuses the colors of the rainbow. In fact, during one of my retreats, after my morning alignment exercises on the beach I returned to my hotel room. Before taking a shower, I lighted a candle to represent the fire element, the opposite polarity to water. When I came out of the shower, I was shocked to see a full circle rainbow around the flame; it displayed the three major colors: red, yellow, and blue. What a phenomenon! I sat on the bed and gazed at it appreciating its beauty and mystery. I felt a sense of oneness and a profound peace. After a while, a minute or two, the rainbow increased in size then slowly faded away.

After reflection, I understood that this was a holographic and symbolic image of my Soul. My mind acted like a prism allowing my inner Light to manifest outward through my optic nerve and then my eyes. Seeing the candle flame, my Soul recognized its own nature and rejoiced in finding the appropriate moment to manifest and demonstrate Cosmic Harmony. And, what better symbol than a rainbow around a burning flame!

In mystical terms, I gave form and made visible the formless and the invisible. If a form dresses the Soul's essence, then this form is alive and expresses itself as art conveying beauty and truth. It is difficult to relate in words such subtle vision of Truth. It was like coming face to face with my Self. This is known as the mystical marriage of Soul with mind, when the two become one.

Spontaneous images appear in connection to what we are thinking or doing at any moment. The purpose is always to join our inner with outer worlds, spiritual with material, invisible with visible, macrocosm with microcosm, actuality with reality, imagination with objectivity. Throughout the years, I have seen many spontaneous apparitions of my Soul inwardly and outwardly, in different forms and colours. Life is truly magical, exciting, and full of wonders and surprises. I love when in the morning while washing my face I see a blue light on the mirror of the bathroom. It confirms my attunement and the Presence of my Soul in my daily life.

My summer retreat of 2010 was exquisite. On the morning of the Egyptian New Year, August 2nd just before dawn, from my balcony I contemplated the rising of Orion and Sirius on the eastern horizon. As

I gazed at the stars, I had the impression that I was in the midst of infinite space. I was imbued with the magic of the moment. Suddenly, I realized that Sirius was between two palm trees. I was shocked and amused at the same time. The symbolism was profound and archetypal. The two palm trees indicated the law of Polarity, similar to the 'pillars' of the Tree of Life, one of the great archetypes based on sacred geometry. The position of Sirius indicated the middle pillar and third point of the trinity. The third point between two opposite polarities always indicates the magical point of balance, harmony, power, and manifestation. I was excited to what it might reveal.

This imagery confirmed that I was on the right track with my search into the Egyptian cosmology mystery in which Orion and Sirius were of prime importance. I knew that it would also involve the initiatory path for my part; because to enter into a mystery means that we are taught and tested as we proceed.

The Orion constellation was higher in the sky. I recalled that the three stars of Orion's belt matched the three pyramids at Giza; hence the Egyptian's axiom, 'As above, so below.' But, what was the representation of Sirius on Earth? I wondered. My morning stellar meeting ended as the eastern horizon began to brighten and the stars slowly faded away. When the Sun rose above the horizon, I made an Egyptian gesture to greet a new day and a New Year.

As I enjoyed my breakfast on the balcony, a turtledove came straight down from the roof with a long sound that was like 'heeeey.' The bird landed right beside me. *'Hey to you too!'* I said with an appreciation for the welcome. I shared my croissant with the bird and so we began what would become a wonderful friendship. The dove is an emblem of the Holy Spirit and of peace, so it was a good sign and a blessing. All birds, from the black sparrow to the white dove, signify thoughts in symbology.

After breakfast, on my way to the beach I saw a mini van with an interesting message on it, 'Live the dream.' I was amused because in mystical terms, it referred to the building of the 'Body of Light.' That is the dream of every mystic. This term is associated with the realm of the Soul, which is light.

When I saw, from afar, the dawn light on the ocean, I rushed to drop my beach bag at my alignment place and dove in the golden dawn light. When I came out of the water, I looked at the Sun and inhaled a deep breath; I held it as long as I could and then slowly exhaled. I repeated this a few times going back in and out of the water. It was a wonderful way to stimulate every blood cell in the body, raise my vibrations, vitalize, and reinforce my aura, the electromagnetic field around the body. When I finished with this exercise, I went on the beach to do my 'Emerald Tablet Exercise.' I stood right in front of the breaking waves. Each time a wave came to my feet, I started the movements to be in sync with the ocean. This is another way to harness the energies, clear the blockages, and create a good circulation. I directed the flow from the feet to the 1st chakra, to the 4th chakra, the heart, and then up to the head, the 7th and crown chakra, opening and activating all the chakras and strengthening the aura. My aura was so strong I could feel it and touch it. After these exercises, I centered all the energies at the heart level and entered into silence to connect mind and Soul. It was truly an inner workout! I lived my dream.

When the aura is strong and magnetized it attracts the positive energies from the environment and acts as a protective shield repelling the negative energy. When the aura is weak, we may feel low, tired, depressed, and overwhelmed. At this critical moment, we may be vulnerable to negative energies. Daily connectedness of Spirit, Soul, and Body is essential for our well-being. The key to speed up our personal transformation is the raising of the vibratory rate of our consciousness and our expression of life.

I went on with my day. I bought a dozen of roses to celebrate the beginning of my retreat. The roses were a good mixture of rainbow colors wrapped with a clear paper on which there was a sticker with 'Freedom' written on it. What a wonderful message! Before going to bed, I set the alarm clock for 5:45 am for my next stellar rendez-vous.

Somehow, I woke up at 5:33. Here was number 33 again! I thought that it was a subliminal call from my Soul. I was excited and rushed out on the balcony. The sky was clear and Sirius was there at the rendez-vous. I sat down to contemplate the majestic rising of Orion and Sirius with an appreciative awareness. Sirius pulsing between the two palm trees seemed to indicate the passageway or gateway to the experience of whatever mystery lies beyond.

I kept in mind the words Sirius and mystery. I recalled a book called 'The Sirius Mystery' by Robert Temple in which he stated that the body of the Sphinx is of a dog not a lion. He went on saying that the head had originally been the head of Anubis but was remolded as a pharaoh's head. Furthermore, he mentioned that the ancient Egyptians spoke often of Anubis in connection with the great pyramids but never of a sphinx. That was it! Anubis/Sphinx was the representation of Sirius on Earth.

The ancient Egyptians venerated Anubis, as the Guardian of the Temple. The great pyramids at Giza were used as magnificent Temples. It all began to make perfect sense. The dog Anubis, as the Guardian of the Temple, stands majestically in front of the pyramids gazing at the eastern horizon waiting for its yearly alignment with the Dog Star Sirius. The connection was so simple and clear. Anubis is Sirius here on Earth. What was truth thousands of years ago is truth today.
I continued with my exploration. What was the purpose and

significance of the connection of the Anubis and Sirius? To find the answer, I had to look at it from a mystical point of view. In ancient Egypt, the great pyramids at Giza were used as a magnificent Temple in which the high initiates or leaders held initiatory ceremonies. They created a dramatic and symbolic representation of divinities. All Egyptian gods and goddesses were representative of divine archetypes for all manifestations on Earth, for the purpose of teaching the natural and spiritual laws of life.

Anubis, the Guardian of the Temple, represented the Gatekeeper who has authority to judge whoever should or should not enter into the Temple. The prerequisite of a candidate was humility. The candidates who were allowed to enter the Temple went through different levels of initiation until they eventually reached illumination and mastership. The structure of the great pyramid provided an energetic environment to that end. The initiations in the King's chamber included vowel sounds; these sounds resonated in the pyramid to create a powerful vibratory force that would trigger the initiate's consciousness into awakening and an expansion of awareness.

The Egyptian sages or high initiates knew that the power of the pyramids existed in terms of time and space. The statue of Anubis gazing at the eastern horizon indicated the ideal time and orientation to align and connect with Sirius. At this precious time, the initiates were allowed to evoke a moment of Cosmic Harmony that would attune the initiate's Soul with the Universal Soul, thus with Eternity.

My morning stellar rendez-vous ended as the Sun rose on the horizon. I was happy and felt satisfied with my new insight into the Egyptian cosmological mystery. I went on with my day taking notes as I continued contemplating the mystery of Anubis.

The Egyptians portrayed Anubis as a black dog with big pointed ears.

Black indicates deep space. The overly large ears may emphasize hearing and communication. By accentuating the ears, did the Egyptians want us to focus our attention on sounds from space? As I was just thinking that, I recalled one of the most extraordinary experiences I had during a retreat. It was August 15, 2004 at 2:06 am, when I was awaken by a strong pulsing sound like a Morse code signal calling for my attention, Pi – Pi – Pi pulsed for quite a while, and then I heard harmonious sounds with different tones; the last one was very low. I put my hands on my ears and could still hear it. Was it from inside or outside? I could not tell the difference. I woke up late that morning and recorded this happening in my notebook.

That day, I went to the beach late in the afternoon. As I strolled along the shore, I asked inwardly, *"What was the signal I heard?"* By the end of my walk, I received enough clues that gave me an understanding. As I entered my hotel room, the digital clock read 7:33 pm. I was amazed. I sat on the couch and heard again the same signal sounds and then the other sounds. I just stayed with it in a receptive state until it stopped. When it let me go, I sat in silence and pondered upon this phenomenon. Was that the 'Music of the Spheres?' I wondered. I was aware that the energy of Cosmic Harmony could be seen as a light or heard as a sound. It depends on our receptivity, either, we are seeing or hearing it; it is the same energy.

The next few days, I received more clues all pointing to Creation, the special time in which we are right now and the global awakening. The clues associated with the signature of the essence behind this phenomenon indicated the Universal Soul and Christ Consciousness. On the last day of my retreat, my girlfriend Judith invited me to join her for an outing; we went to the Four Seasons Hotel. They had a charming restaurant on a terrace overlooking the ocean. As we were ready to go, we went closer to the beach to appreciate the beautiful panorama, when suddenly a magnificent rainbow appeared over the ocean. What a wonderful sign of universal Love! When we drove back home, in front of us there was a car with a license plate with the numbers 888. That was for me the ultimate confirmation. As we have seen in the previous chapter, 888 is the mystical code of Jesus Christ.

Concerning the Music of the Spheres, Pythagoras, Greek philosopher and mathematician, said that he heard it. This revelation assisted him in the discovery of harmonic ratios of sounds in relation to the planetary spheres and their correspondences, music notes, numbers, colors and chemical elements. Music was for him an art and science that revealed the law of harmonic intervals. Later on, Plato took this concept one step further and related it to the structure of the Universe, the order and harmony of the Cosmos. Both, Pythagoras and Plato, were initiated in the Temples of Egypt.

Modern day theories of physicists are in accordance with ancient Wisdom Traditions, which claim the holographic interconnectedness of the Universe. Ancient Masters stated that the Universe was a harmonious creation designed by the Creator, the Divine Being. Moreover, they emphasized that God is Love. The energy of Divine Love – the Word of God – is the creative life force that can be seen as light, heard as sound, or felt as an airstream, the Holy Breath or Holy Spirit. The whole Universe, seen and unseen, is composed of a network of energy underlying the order and harmony of the Universe.

My retreat 2010 ended with more revelations, confirmations, and signatures concerning the Master Soul of this new era. My last retreat of 2011 was as delightful. From the balcony, I continued contemplating the rising of Sirius between the two palm trees with an appreciative awareness of the importance of this event.

Throughout the years, I realized that the structure of the holographic Universe allows instantaneous communication between Nature, Humanity, and the Universe. Since it is through harmony and resonance that energy, light and sound, is transmitted from one level of consciousness to another.

Sometimes during my retreats in Palm Beach I would receive an intuitive feeling to take a picture. When I took the picture below, there were no clouds in the sky. All I could see was the pure radiance of the Sun with rays of light spreading in different directions. I was hoping that it would capture a geometric form. And it did! After the development, I was amazed to see the form of a pyramid with the Sun on its apex. I wondered if the image was due to a dysfunction of my camera. Or was it a UFO or a holographic image of a pyramid? Archetypal images have a holographic quality and fundamental teachings.

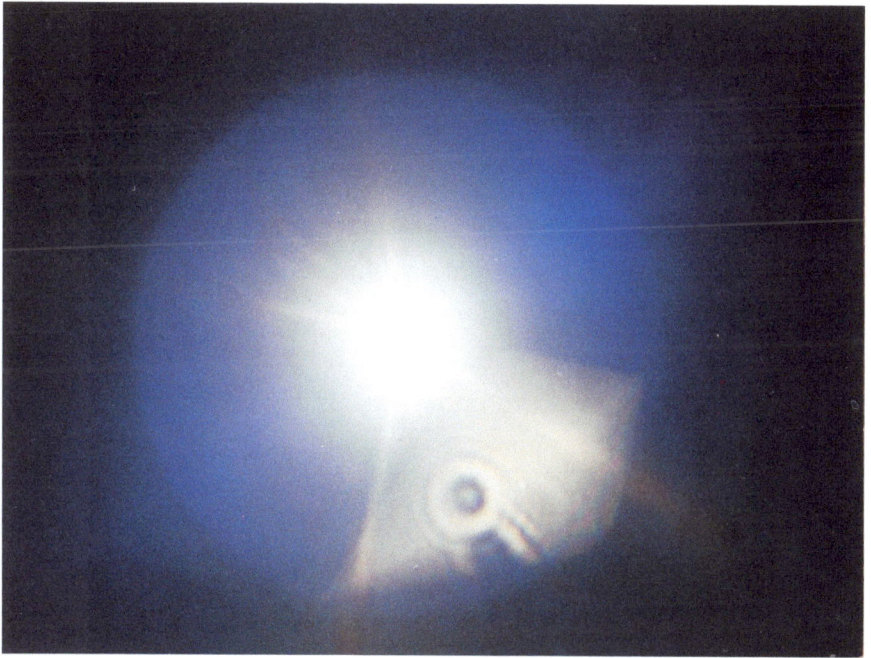

Pyramid of Light

Gateway & Gatekeeper

A gateway is an entrance, a door or way into the experience of whatever mystery lies beyond the gate. Every gateway has its gatekeeper. There are gateways in sacred architecture like the Egyptian Temples, Solomon's Temple or the Gothic cathedrals. There are gateways in Nature, on the surface of Earth called landscapes, and in the sky, the planets, and stars.

The gateway and the gatekeeper have great significance; both are spiritual Presences or Angels. An angel is a spiritual aspect of the One God. The gatekeeper, the guardian of the place or sanctuary, has authority and judges whoever should or should not enter the gate. The requirements are a strong love and humility. As we make ourselves ready for entry through purification of mind and give a password that our heart dictates, the gate opens. The gatekeeper appears through psychological attunement or even sometimes physically through an outside agent, either way the gatekeeper is always present within us. The gatekeeper questions our intentions, converses and even cheers us. We may develop a relationship with the gatekeeper to receive words of wisdom, encouragements, and clues of the way ahead. Through the gatekeeper, we may converse and walk with God hand in hand, receiving guidance, encouragement, and confirmation as to what is best to do, where to go, and when it is the best time.

When the Sun rises or sets on the horizon, it marks a gateway to what lies beyond. The Sun's gatekeeper is the mediator between Heaven and Earth. He is the mid-point point of balance and harmony. In the system of the Wheel of Time and Space, each solar power point marks a gateway.

The Gatekeeper

In Christianity, the supreme Gatekeeper is Jesus Christ who said succinctly, *"I am the door, the entrance into the kingdom." – "Seek and you shall find." — "Knock and it shall be opened unto you." – "Ask and you shall be given." – "I am the Way, the Truth, and the Life."*

Nowadays, many people do not come and knock at the door; neither do they know how to ask for assistance in a simple and direct way. They do not even understand the workings of natural and spiritual laws involved in the process, even though the teachings have been given by the Masters thousands of years ago. What a sad and pathetic state of mind.

A true Christian is one who searches, discovers, and practices Truth. Christianity has derived its name from *Christos*, a Greek word for 'Divine Consciousness' which is also Divine Love and Truth. The

Divine Being who said, "I AM the Way, the Truth, and the Life" guided us toward a simple, beautiful *Way* of service, toward an understanding and knowledge of *Truth* and toward a *Life* of sharing and loving.

Peter Dawkins, a recognized authority on the Western Wisdom Traditions, author of many books, explains in his book, 'The Great Vision,' in the section of the Judaic-Christian Mysteries, the path of Initiation that Jesus came to teach in order to guide humanity on the path of evolution towards the sublime Light. Peter informs us:

> "What the Christ Jesus portrayed for us, in his incarnation as Jesus of Nazareth, was the initiatory path of every man from beginning to end; and to do this he acted out dramatically, in real life situations, the actual symbols and allegorical stories, that were used in the Temples and Schools of the Mysteries during preceeding Ages.... Jesus gave the world a living picture book by means of which to see the Christ and the divine processes of life..." Peter continued saying, "Jesus Christ lived as Jesus of Nazareth in order to show vividly to mankind the Way, Truth and Life of God, and in such way that every man could have the chance to identify with and hence attempt to follow this great Example. Jesus not only spoke and interpreted the Truth with his voice, but with his very actions, his deeds or works being the principal witness of his state of being."

On the path of Initiation, a true Christian is one who has passed the 3rd initiation 'Crucifixion' which has to do with the surrender and death of the ego. The gatekeeper waits for us at the threshold of the 4th initiation, 'Resurrection' which is associated with the heart, if allowed to pass then we emerge into higher life and consciousness. The heart is the place of balance, harmony, beauty, joy, power, and manifestation. It is at this level that the Christ within becomes active and made known. To see, hear and know the Christ within is to see, hear and know Jesus Christ. *"Blessed are the pure in heart, for they shall see God."*

By following the path of Initiation, we follow the footsteps of Jesus; step by step we move closer to the sublime Light. This is what Christianity means – to make the effort to live consciously and truly, to follow the guidance of the Soul and to remain true to our Self, to God. As we work on our spirituality, we develop a greater consciousness in ourselves and gain more understanding of what life is all about.

From an excerpt of an Egyptian text, a candidate arrived in front of the door of the sanctuary and knocked. The gatekeeper appeared and asked questions. After the correct answers were given, the door opened and the candidate was allowed to enter. In this testimonial text, we can hear the candidate's joy.

> *"O Lord of Manifestations,*
> *Great and majestic.*
> *Here I have come!*
> *And the Hereafter for me has opened up.*
> *The paths in Heaven, the paths on Earth,*
> *For me have opened,*
> *And there is no one to oppose me!"*

The candidate passed the threshold and was infused with the Divine Light. From that moment the initiate's Soul was in resonance with the Universal Soul. It is a precious moment when an initiate is born – a star is born! The initiate has reached the first step of illumination, became an adept and was on the way to his or her mastership.

Everyone following the footsteps of the Masters and the guidance of their own Soul, the Master Within, will eventually reach illumination and sing the song of joy. In doing so quickly and with a clear mind, the pressure from on High will be less intense; hence, we can avoid unnecessary sufferings and struggles in our lives. I believe that in the new Age and Golden Age in which we are now entering, many will pass the threshold. This is known as the Second Coming. It is encouraging to know that the Christ within, in the heart Soul of each one of us, is lovingly waiting for our coming so that we may return to the Source of Life as illuminated beings.

The First Coming relates to the good Shepherd or Christ Soul who comes down to Earth to teach and guide us through initiation, until we become conscious of the Christ within our Soul. To see, hear, and know the Christ within is to see, hear, and know Jesus Christ. This state of being constitutes the Second Coming.

The image of the rising Sun above the horizon is a constant reminder that after the darkness of the night, the light always comes and rises shining its radiance and glory for all to see and behold. During my retreats, when I dive in the ocean, float or bath in the dawn light, I do this to purify myself, embody more light and become at-one with that Light. It is a wonderful inner workout! The Sun's dawn light represents both an individual's Soul and the Universal Soul dawning.

The Great Angel or Gatekeeper of the Sun's sphere is the Christ who is the Lord of its Dawn Light. The dawn light is associated with the coming of the divine Light, the coming of Jesus Christ.

On the cosmological level, when Venus rises on the eastern horizon just before the Sun, they both represent the 'Morning Star." When Sirius rises once a year on the eastern horizon, the three form a trinity and all three become the 'Morning Star' which is associated with Christ Jesus in His descent to our world in order to bring more Light, more Love and Life to it.

Master Souls

A Master Soul is one who is illuminated by the Christ Spirit. The title of Christ is given to one who is illumined in the fullest sense possible with the Light of God. All Master Souls form the Christ Consciousness, also known as the Heavenly Jerusalem. The non-Christian mystics prefer to use the term of Cosmic Consciousness because it is universal and represent the Masters of all Traditions. There is but One Soul – the Soul of God, the Universal Soul wherein the Master Souls watch over us. There are many illuminated Beings or Master Souls connected with our planetary evolution, each having a purpose to fulfill.

The Master Soul we know as Jesus Christ was given different names by various Wisdom Traditions. One of the oldest biblical names was Enoch or Atlas, King of Atlantis. The ancient Egyptians knew him as Thoth. The Greeks called him Christos or Hermes and the Romans knew him as Mercury. In Islamic Tradition, he is known as Idris, and in eastern Tradition as Babaji or Shiva. They are all names in different Traditions for the same Great Teacher and Master Soul who appears to us again and again throughout the millenniums to teach and initiate us into the mysteries of life, and guide us on our path of evolution towards the sublime Light.

Peter Dawkins, a recognized authority on the Western Wisdom Traditions, explains in his book, 'The Great Vision,' the connection between Sirius and the Great Master Souls. In this incredible book, Peter reveals profound truths about the Master Souls and their missions. In the section entitled "Jesus and His Christ Mission" Peter informs us:

"The Soul that we know as Jesus, who lived approximately two thousands years ago as Jesus of Nazareth, is historically one of those truly great Souls that we call Christs, Sons of God, for such great Souls have reached (as far as we are concerned) a divine perfection and are actively manifesting the Christ Light. There are many Master Souls connected to our planetary evolution, all of them beautifully illumined beings, but the greatness of the Jesus Soul that we call the Christ (Soul) for our world surpasses them all. It is said that his Soul achieved perfection in worlds other than our own, and that he is a Great Initiate of the star system called Sirius, the evolution of which is far beyond our own. From the great Christ Brotherhood of Sirius he came with two others on a special mission to our solar system, entering it via the Sun, its heart, and then incarnating into the coarse environment of our planetary sphere…"

The two other Master Souls from Sirius joining Jesus were Moses and Elias, as we know them in the Judaic-Christian Mysteries. They form the Trinity-in-Unity that manifests the three aspects of the Cosmic Christ. This universal Truth transcends any human dogma or limited understanding, and needs to be approached with humility and an intelligent open mindedness.

A Master Soul always appears in periods of transition, at the end of an Age, to help, inspire and support humanity through the difficult times, and to ground the new impulse for the new Age. Christ, the supreme Great Lord has been with this world since its beginning, manifesting whenever appropriate throughout the Ages.

On the picture below, the Sun was behind a thick cloud. After development, I was surprised to see a man's face looking up at the Sun. The face stamped in the cloud could be a thought-form of a Master Soul.

Face in the Cloud

Star Light

Many years ago, I was invited to a Yoga Center in Los Angeles. My friend Aviva asked me to join in their New Year celebration. I had never been in an eastern Tradition center before, so I was excited to meet this group. As I entered the room, some musicians were playing ancient soft music to soothe our modern minds. The atmosphere was pleasant. When the lights were dimmed in the room, a live broad cast appeared on the screen. A woman speaker welcomed us with a cheerful voice. I was relaxed and listening carefully to her speech when suddenly a big star light appeared in the corner of the room. I was stunned. Because there were no exclamatory reactions from the audience, I thought perhaps they were familiar with this projection of the star light, which may have been used for the New Year ambiance. The star light was so beautiful and inspiring. I wanted to buy this star light system or projector.

The woman on the screen went on with her discourse but for me her voice was fading away. My mind was mesmerized. I could not keep my eyes off the star light. At the end of the speech, the lights of the room were turned on and the star light disappeared. There were plenty of hugs among the people. It was nice to see the camaraderie. My friend Aviva was cheerful and came to give me a big hug.

"Did you like it?" She asked me.
"I am very grateful you invited me. That was quiet an experience. Where can I buy the star light projector? I asked her.
"What star light projector?" She replied.

I was surprised at her response. I explained that I saw a big star light in the room and had enjoyed it throughout the speech. She turned around and asked other people if they had seen it. To my surprise, no one else had seen it. I was puzzled. We then went to the bookstore of the Center. Instantly, I was attracted to a golden notebook titled, 'Trust'. As I held it in my hands, I felt a warm feeling of love in my heart. What a wonderful confirmation and encouragement. *"In God I trust."* I said inwardly.

That evening, I decoded the word 'trust.' Its numeric value was 93. Number 9 corresponds to the letter 'I' or 'J' and number 3 to the letter 'C'. I concentrated on the 'I' and 'C' and simply translated the letters as

'I see.' I knew that number 93 was also the numeric value of the word, 'good,' which is synonymous with 'God.' I did not need to go any further that was a message and reminder to trust in God. I was convinced that the star light apparition was a vision of Truth, a revelation of the eternal Light.

The next day Aviva called me to say that she had talked with a longtime member who told her that in the past, every so often, someone in the audience had seen a star light in that same room. I was pleased to hear that and grateful that I had the privilege to witness it.

"What do you think it was?" she asked.
"The Presence of a Master Soul." I replied with conviction.

We continued conversing on this subject and the wondrous workings of the holographic Universe.

Many years have passed since the unforgettable appearance of the star light at the Yoga Center. Each time when I look up at the stars, I send my love to all the Master Souls who have guided humanity throughout the centuries and still do.

2012 & Beyond

We are right now living in a momentous and exciting time. Throughout the centuries and even millenniums, Masters of all Traditions have nurtured humanity toward this extraordinary yet challenging time in which we are right now. As we approach the famous and critical date of December 21, 2012, humanity's consciousness is being hastened into a higher evolutionary state. To understand what is happening and discover what the Masters prophesized for humanity, we need to look at this great event on a cosmological and spiritual level.

Cosmological Level

Earth and the Sun are in a rare alignment with the heart center of the Milky Way. This alignment is calculated when the Sun's ecliptic and the equator of the Milky Way cross each other at the solstices. This celestial alignment opens up a channel from the heart of the Milky Way to the Sun and then to the Earth.

What is important to know is that through this channel, waves of cosmic super-rays downpour on the Sun causing extra solar activity, which in turn affects Earth's electro-magnetic field and climate. However, let us not think that it will be the end of the world.

According to ancient Wisdom and modern astronomers, we are right now entering into a new Age and a new Great Age. To the ancient Egyptians, the Great Age was known as 'Zep tepi' it literally means the 'First Time' because it was associated with Creation and the beginning of Time.

Robert Bauval mentioned in his new book, 'The Egypt Code' that between the paws of the Sphinx/Anubis there is a stela, a large stone, with encoded instructions. One line reads, "This is the splendid place of the First Time." The First Time is associated with the beginning of Time and the Great Age. Here lies a great mystery that could help us understand the relation of the stars Orion and Sirius with the new Age and the new Great Age in which we are now entering.

To the Mayans, the Great Age was associated with the end of the Fourth World and the beginning of the Fifth World, humanity's next evolutionary phase. Their Long Count calendar gives what is believed to be the date of December 21, 2012, for this transition. The Mayans wisely left unsaid any prediction. However, they did mention that the transition would probably be difficult and dangerous. Of course, that is because the future of humanity depends on our freewill, goodwill and our imagination. We have to create our future or rather co-create it with Nature and the Master Souls.

Peter Dawkins, expert in Western Wisdom Traditions and Cosmology, questioned and commented on this subject of the new Age and great new Age.

> "But where does the zodiacal division of the ecliptic begin and end? How do we know when each Age, or a Great Age, begins and ends? Because the stars are in slow but continual motion, they can only be taken as approximate aids in marking the divisions of the ecliptic and hence of time. However, there are two fixed markers. These are the two points on the ecliptic where the equator of the Milky Way galaxy (our galaxy) crosses the ecliptic."

Peter used a graphic to show this alignment and the new positions of the Zodiac signs. For those who would like more information on this subject, please go to his website: www.zoence.com/article/the-great-ages and www.zoence.com/article/zodiac-of-ages.

On the Spiritual Level
We are living in an extraordinary time. To begin with, it is important to understand that the whole solar system is moving into a more highly charged part of the Milky Way, and that it is receiving exceptionally high pulses of energy from the heart of the Milky Way.

Since our whole being is in resonance with this great wave, it affects us on all the levels: physical, mental, emotional, and spiritual. It is something to be extremely grateful for because it can help us raise our vibrations, clear our mind, speed up our personal transformation and accelerate the evolutionary process of our consciousness. As the world's transformation speeds up, we are experiencing a great cleansing and rebalancing on a personal, national, and global level. More than ever, it is important to keep our aura strong and remain centered in our own Soul.

Peter Dawkins ended his comments about the Great Age by saying:

> "From the spiritual point of view these times are associated with the two baptisms: the first by water and the second by air and fire (i.e. the Holy Breath or Spirit). From the physical point of view it causes great changes, difficulties and challenges, with destructions and mutations of species, including the human race. They are major initiatory moments. We are experiencing one right now. At the start of a Great Age this is when the galactic heart is aligned with the midwinter solstice sun — the Christmas or Birthday of a Great Age. The old Phoenix dies and is reborn, renewed, resurrecting from the ashes of its old form."

Throughout the Ages, the Masters knew that this great wave would offer us an incredible opportunity for a collective spiritual awakening. They also knew that this great event would precipitate a major crisis for humanity. This crisis is due to a dark psychological phase that we all must pass through just before our spiritual awakening. The Masters chose the Phoenix to symbolize the alchemical process of this transition in which the old Phoenix dies and is reborn, resurrecting from the ashes of its old form.

On the pattern of Initiation the death of the Phoenix refers to the 3rd initiation. This initiation is called 'Crucifixion' and is associated with the Fire element. It concerns the surrender and death of ego. It is a psychological death, a let go of the ego's attachments and illusions. Ancient philosophers, poets, and mystics all described this dark psychological phase as 'The Dark Night of the Soul.' It concerns the surrendering of the ego and to make one's will according to the Will of God, of Love; thus, learning to love in a divine way and live truly.

The Dark Night of the Soul is a blessing in disguise, because it strengthens the heart, tests the intentions, and speeds up the process of transformation. It is encouraging to know that as soon as we surrender the ego the Dark Night ends and the divine Light infuses us and blesses us with loving illumination and prosperity.

In eastern Traditions, the Maha Mantra: 'I surrender to you, O Lord' refers to this difficult 3rd initiation. It is a method of attuning the mind and heart directly on God. This state of being brings one to the threshold of the 4th initiation, 'Resurrection' associated with the heart. The Gatekeeper standing on the horizon's line between Heaven and Earth waits for our coming. If we have learned well our lessons, made the necessary changes and reached sufficient purity of the mind, then and only then, the Gatekeeper allows us to pass and emerge into higher life and consciousness. This state of being constitutes the Second Coming.

As we move closer to the date of December 21, 2012, the theme of 'The Dark Night of the Soul' will intensify throughout the year and the years to come. People who do not understand what is going on in this critical time, and are not making the necessary efforts and changes in their lifestyle are experiencing intense inner and outer conflicts, unnecessary struggles and sufferings; all due to their resistance and endless rounds of avoidable karmic lessons. These people need to take time out to evaluate their situations, adjust or reinvent themselves in order to be in tune with the higher energy of the new Age; otherwise a severe correction or a burnout will occur affecting their health and lifestyle. This self-examination will prove to be far more important than any busy work that keeps them occupied and cut off from the creative flow of life.

Millions of people around the world have prepared themselves for this celestial alignment. They have made the necessary changes and reached sufficient purity of mind. These people are already receiving the stimulation of the influx of energies of the new Age. They are able to experience more timeless moments, as they become more and more enlightened. These are the people, from around the world, who are working on establishing a Golden Age in which the materialistic mentality with its selfishness and corruption has no place and will be undermined. Dictatorship governments around the world are already collapsing, as people demand justice and freedom. It is comforting to know that the Masters have prophesized for humanity that this new Age will be a Golden Age of freedom, harmony, wisdom, prosperity, peace and joy.

As humanity enters into the new era, we begin to see more enlightened leaders working towards a united global humanity in which balanced and just societies can flourish. It has already begun.

Freedom

When we follow the guidance of the Soul, we are free to flow with life. We are free to be loving and strong. We are free to dream yet be realistic, focused, and organized. We can be idealistic and practical. When we reach this level of consciousness and resonance, it is at that moment that we become truly human. We begin to comprehend how an abstract conception of our Soul generates ideas and gives form to the ideals of life.

Unfortunately, today's fast pace of life and busyness disturb our balance and well-being. In fact, it suppresses individuality, creativity, and freedom. The world today is overwhelmed with economic and social problems. We may think that reactions such as defensiveness, conflict, anger, frustration, struggle, anxiety, confusion, and fear are all attributes of living. Yet is this really living? Two thousands years ago, Jesus said, *"Look at the slavery of your life."* What would He says to us today?

Since we perceive the world in our own minds, we perceive in terms of thought. By thinking that we are a body, a job, a drama and believing that we are the masks we wear in society, we are still slaves. We live in the illusions of the ego and believe them to be true. What a sad and pathetic state of mind.

Because reality is an inner experience projected outward, if our thoughts are negative, we will perceive them in the outer world. What we perceive is our own inner conflicts, shadows, turmoil, and illusions, which are all of our own making. This may prove to be a vicious and an endless circle of karmic lessons. In ignorance, we demand and expect things from life and others. When we live in this illusionary world or are trapped in it, it deceives us by creating unnecessary sufferings, struggles, desperation, confusion, diseases, and unhappiness. By becoming more self-conscious and aware, we can reclaim ourselves and change our perceptions of things. When the mind dwells on depressive and anxious thoughts, we attract the very conditions we would like to avoid. The axiom, 'like attracts like' is very true. At anytime, we have the power to shift our realities. The Soul requires that we stop identifying ourselves with the ego and start living a truer lifestyle.

In everyday life, it is essential that our thoughts are positive and constructive if we desire to attract beneficent responses and influences. With a genuine confidence, which is an intense trust in our Soul, not an assumed confidence which is just a blind faith or belief, we can start to live a truer life that is often accompanied by experiences of humility, kindness, gratitude, creativity, enthusiasm, joy and peace.

In the wintertime, Palm Beach is a renowned international playground for the rich and famous, and the not so famous. This charming small town becomes a crowded Shakespearean stage upon which all the psychological subpersonalities or roles are played. Yet, Palm Beach is reputed to be a place of 'Good Life.' It depends upon one's understanding of what is good, what is life, and what life is all about. And, if one is truly free.

Life is good when we experience the Soul's qualities of light, love, and freedom. We are truly free when we remain true to God. Three thousands years ago, Pharaoh Akhenaton discovered this profound truth and chose the motto, 'Living in Truth.' In living a creative life, we discover new ways to think and new ways to respond that enable us to live on a higher level of consciousness even in this tumultuous world. In this state of being, we discover a new way of living that offers love, freedom, happiness, prosperity, and peace of mind.

3 Steps to Freedom

1. Willingness – "I am willing …"
When we are willing to let go of the obstacles of impossibilities and obligations, we are ready to take action to free ourselves. We are willing to be open to creative life and experience what life brings us. We are willing to experience the gifts of life just as they are. We are willing to experience the Soul's qualities of light, love, and freedom. Our willingness brings us to the second step of freedom.

2. Gratitude – "I am grateful …"
Our gratitude can open us to experience the law of Attraction, when we express gratitude not just a simple thank you for help or a gift received, but a sincere thank you from deep down in our heart. The exchange between the giver and receiver releases a powerful energy that attracts the positive energy from our environment; hence, we experience prosperity in all things. In this state of being, we develop a

magnetic personality that attracts the very best in life. Our gratitude brings us to the third step of freedom.

3. Joy – "I am enjoying …"
True life is meant for our enjoyment. When we enjoy life, we live in the moment and expand our consciousness. The more we enjoy life, the more we appreciate its harmony, beauty, and power. There is nothing greater than to enjoy the divine Presence within us and within each other. Joy lights up our life. The radiance of joy intensifies our aura and the aura of the world. When we are joyful, we radiate the Soul's quality of light, love, and freedom. When we find joy, we find our paradise here on Earth.

Our willingness to experience gratitude and joy sets us free!

Appendix 1

The Wheel of Time & Space

Time manifests in our realities through a geometric pattern of light lines, which repeats in endless cycles giving us the illusion of linear time. Time on Earth is relative to our planet and its revolving movement around the Sun, which creates a circle of space. Time and space might be illusions of the objective mind, but not illusions to be denied for they are essential in the evolution of the human consciousness.

The problem is knowing the right thing to do, when and where and how to begin. It can not be done without some structure. We need a system of orientation to align our inner and outer worlds. In Ancient Wisdom, the basic structure of the cycle of time was known as the Wheel of Life, the Wheel of Karma, the Wheel of Fortune and Destiny, and the Medicine Wheel.

 Knowing that my spiritual retreats and mystical experiences were synchronized with time and space, I followed diligently the 'apparent' path of the Sun because there is a rhythm in Nature and the Universe that can support us and assist us to elevate our mind and speed up our personal transformation. Throughout the years, I developed a yearly program to be in tune with the rhythm of Nature and the Universe.

Each year is a solar cycle in which there are 8 solar power points. Each of these solar power points is a vortex of energy like a chakra in Time.

Each one marks a gateway. Each solar power point has its own quality, purpose, and influence on our life. When we attune ourselves with these solar power points and with awareness of what they represent, we empower ourselves and allow the process of life and time to work for us instead of against us. Going with the creative flow of life can be extremely uplifting, healing, vitalizing, rejuvenating, and enlightening bringing happiness, fulfillment, and prosperity in our material and spiritual lives.

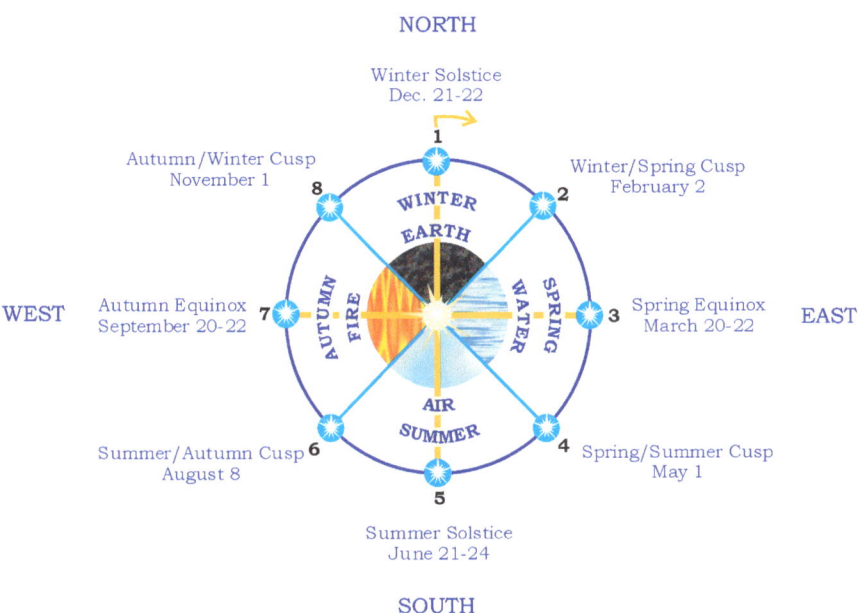

The Wheel of Time and Space

The 8 solar power points are marked by the solstices, equinoxes, and the cusps of the season, when a season starts and another ends. The cycle of Nature has 4 cardinal points, 4 seasons and 4 elements. As we follow the path of the Sun, the movement is clockwise from the north to the east, to the south and then to the west. Knowing this gives us the right time and right orientation to align ourselves with the creative flow of life.

Between each power point there are approximately 6 to 7 weeks, giving us plenty of time for assimilation, application, and preparation for the next solar power point influences, urges, and opportunities. It is like surfing the waves of time!

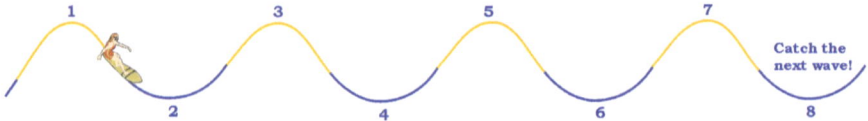

The Waves of Time

The solar power points of the solstices and the equinoxes are marked by the yellow curves indicating a favorable time for opportunities and celebrations. The blue curves mark the most critical times of the year when we might feel low, tired, depressed, and most vulnerable. During these blue periods, it is a time for evaluation and meditation. These are times of testing yet of empowerment! With knowledge and awareness, we can avoid unnecessary sufferings and struggles, cancel karmic lessons to free ourselves and enjoy a smooth ride with God's blessings.

The yearly program consists of taking each solar power point at a time. Each has within its own ten topics:

1. Orientation, Season & Element
This aligns us to the direction of each power point and tunes us in with the season and its element. With the right orientation, we can energize our prayers, meditations, and spiritual exercises.

2. What is happening in Nature?
This section relates to the seasonal influences in relation to natural and human life.

3. How it affects our life?
This speaks of the influences of the elements, earth, water, air, and fire,

which affect our physical, emotional, mental, and spiritual states.

4. In Terms of Positive and Negative
Depending on how we react to seasonal influences, we may experience them in a positive or negative way. The elements of the period can influence us and urge us to work on our spirituality, recognize and seize each opportunity that comes our way. We can choose to experience life in a constructive and enjoyable way or in a destructive and painful way. It is up to us!

5. What we can do?
This section empowers us with knowledge letting us know how we can make the influences work for us instead of against us.

6. The Festival of the period
Many Traditions have festivals throughout the year. These festivals have the ability to nourish, heal, inspire, and uplift especially when they are celebrated consciously in harmony with the rhythm of time. Each Festival has its own topic.

7. On the Path of Initiation
The path of initiation is the 'way' to enlightenment. This section indicates how the element of the season affects our spiritual development and intensifies the karmic lessons we encounter during each period. Guidance is given on how we may recognize these lessons and how to cancel them. That is the only way to light up our life and create realities that are more enjoyable and lasting.

8. Sub Personality or Role
There are many sub personalities and roles that we may activate and play during any given period. Each represents different aspects of the human psyche. Each one has its own style and motivation of its own. "All the world's a stage, and the men and women merely players." Shakespeare.

9. Symbols of the period

Symbols speak to our intellect and emotions and convey information about our inner psychological and spiritual world. A symbol allows us to discover hidden truths that have the power to alter our consciousness. For this reason, some symbols related to the period have been chosen and are explained with a brief mystical point of view.

10. Tarot Cards of the period

In this work, the Tarot system is used as spiritual psychology, which has nothing to do with fortunetellers. The Tarot is an ancient science and one of the oldest games used in the Mystery Schools of Egypt. The game captures the influences at work, reveals profound truths, and conveys valuable and insightful information. Each solar power point has two complementary Tarot cards; each card represents a guiding archetype. A brief mystical interpretation is given for each card.

Tarot in Latin is 'Rota' meaning rotation, the turning motion of the Wheel of Life. In ancient Egypt, the name Tarosh or Tarot meant the Royal Way – the Way to Enlightenment.

The Wheel of Time and Space with its program supports and assists us throughout the year. The system opens up a new resource of increased intuition, creative insight, solutions to problems for the achievement of our highest goals and successes in our work or business, leading to a steady and fulfilling way of life, lasting happiness and peace of mind.

The complete program is available on my website: www.atoneforever.com.

Appendix 2

The Emerald Tablet Exercise

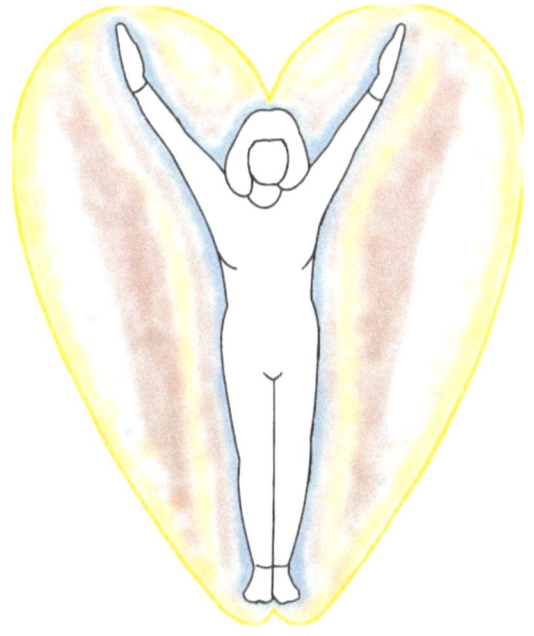

Just before I began my spiritual retreat in 1996, I translated the ancient Egyptian 'Emerald Tablet' formula knowing that it was an alchemical formula of regeneration. Alchemy is the chemistry of the 'All' or whole being: physical, emotional, mental and spiritual. The Egyptians stated succinctly, 'As above so below, as below so above, for the doing of the Great Work.' Above is Heaven, below is you on Earth.

I converted the formula into an exercise of a series of gentle yet powerful movements to establish balance and harmony within and reinforce the aura. When the aura is strong and magnetized, it glorifies the creative power within, attracts positive energies from the environment, and acts as a protective shield. On the other hand, when the aura is weak, we may feel low, tired, depressed, and overwhelmed. At that critical moment, we may be vulnerable to negative energies from others and ours; hence, we create unnecessary struggles and sufferings. The key to speed up our personal transformation is the raising of our vibrations. Daily connectedness of Spirit, Soul, and Body is essential for our well-being.

The Emerald Tablet Exercise has two parts. The first part consists of stirring and removing blockages in order to create a good circulation of energy to establish balance and harmony within ourselves. The second part consists of centering and unifying all the energies at the heart chakra and connecting mind and Soul. Throughout the exercise, we use our breath and focus on the movement to direct the energy flow. It is truly an inner workout! The exercise opens and activates all the chakras and strengthens the aura.

An understanding, focus, breathing and gentle powerful movements are all a part of this exercise which takes only 5 to 10 minutes. An understanding that this system works on all levels of consciousness is essential.

Part 1

The movement starts from below, the ground, to harness the energy of Earth, then we bring it up to the 1st chakra, continue to the heart, the 4th chakra, and then above the head, the 7th chakra. The flow of energies then burst out and arches on each side of the body to fall back to the ground like a fountain of clear water. We repeat this part 4 to 7 times, in doing so the movement creates a heart shape aura pulsing with love; hence, one becomes the opposite polarity to Heaven and attracts Spirit energy.

Part 2

The second part consists of unifying all the levels at the heart chakra. Through a special visualization and affirmation, the mind is connected with the Soul, the source of inspiration, intuition, and insights. This connection relates to the sublimation of the Great Work in which the vibratory rate of our consciousness is elevated. This speeds up our personal transformation into something higher, more refined, and sublime. When mind and Soul blend together we become at one forever. In so doing we bring more light in our life and build our 'Body of Light.' The realm of the Soul is called the 'Body of Light' because it is made of spiritual Æther, which is Light, also known as the Quintessence or Fifth element.

On my website, I will have a section for the Emerald Tablet Exercise in which the whole exercise will be explained with graphics and videos.

Appendix 3

The Baconian Keyboard

Since ancient times, letters and numbers have been used to represent abstract ideas. Every letter of the alphabet is actually a symbol deriving from an archetype with a numerical value and spiritual meaning. Such symbolism has the power to convey information and alter our consciousness. A symbol is not an end in itself but a means to an end.

The purpose of using any system should be to maintain daily connection between mind and Soul. The decoding of letters and numbers encourages an inner dialogue and the development of loving devotion that can transfer consciousness to higher awareness. The key to understand and unlock the hidden meaning of a word, name or message, and release their energy power is to be able to recognize, decode and interpret the symbolism and its hidden message.

The Baconian Keyboard is named after Sir Francis Bacon, English philosopher of the 17th century and leader of the Rosicrucians. Francis Bacon created many different systems of letters and numbers. I personally use only one of his systems, which I called 'The Baconian Keyboard.' It is based on 24 letters of the alphabet wherein each letter has an equivalent numerical value from A 1 to Z 24. Two letters I and U share the same space column with J and V. There are three variations: the Simple Cipher, the Reverse Cipher, and the Kay Cipher.

	A	B	C	D	E	F	G	H	I/J	K	L	M	N	O	P	Q	R	S	T	U/V	W	X	Y	Z
SIMPLE	1	2	3	4	5	6	7	8	9	10	11	12	13	14	15	16	17	18	19	20	21	22	23	24
REVERSE	24	23	22	21	20	19	18	17	16	15	14	13	12	11	10	9	8	7	6	5	4	3	2	1
KAY	25	26	27	28	29	30	31	32	33	10	11	12	13	14	15	16	17	18	19	20	21	22	23	24

The numeral value of a word is derived by the addition of the letter values. Word values can then be used separately or added together to unlock the coded meaning of a word, a name or signature, a date, a symbol or a myth. The Baconian Keyboard can help us discover messages, guidance, and correspondences between different systems like the Tree of Life, the Wheel of Time and Space, the Chakras and Tarot systems among others.

You can begin using the Simple Cipher to decode your own initials and full name to discover the numeric value. Each time you see these numbers pop up; they will put you instantly in touch with your Soul, to receive guidance, confirmation, and encouragement.

Throughout this book, I gave plenty of examples on how the system can be used. I suggest that you make a list of words that relates to yourself and your spiritual studies. Then you can discover the numeric value and the interrelation with other corresponding systems. You will be surprise at what it may reveal.

Further Reading

As you have seen through this book, the path of Initiation is extremely important in the development of our spirituality and in speeding up our personal transformation. On my spiritual retreats, I always had with me three books concerning the pattern of Initiation, all from Peter's work. Peter Dawkins is a recognized authority on the Western Wisdom Traditions.

The Pattern of Initiation in the Evolution of Human Consciousness.
It covers the Eleusinian and Dionysian Mysteries – The Great Instauration of Light – The Winters Tale – Symbols of the Ladder of Initiation.

The Great Vision
The first part of the book covers the pattern of Initiation and the Christian Mysteries.

Arcadia – Studies in Ancient Wisdom
The first part of the book covers the pattern of Initiation and the Ancient Egyptian Mysteries.

The Tempest from the series of The Wisdom of Shakespeare by Peter Dawkins.

All Peter's books are available on his website: www.zoence.com - In the 'Info Sheets' of this website you will find the Tree of Life and the Chakra systems.

Other books of interest:
Mental Alchemy by Ralph M. Lewis
Marriage of the Mind by George F. Buletza
The Mystical Life of Jesus by H. Spencer Lewis
The Secret Teachings of All Ages by Manly Hall
The Secret Language of Symbols by David Fontana
The Dictionary of Symbols by Jean Chevalier and Alain Gheerbrant

www.ingramcontent.com/pod-product-compliance
Lightning Source LLC
Chambersburg PA
CBHW042315150426
43201CB00001B/8